How to use this book

This is a book about common things that may be seen at the seaside. It is an outline natural history of the edge of the sea—of the water itself, the shores, sand, mud, shingle and rocky cliffs—and of the marvellously varied populations of plants and animals that live there. The coast is here treated as a series of habitats, or zones, from exposed rocky shores, through sandy or muddy ones, to estuaries and harbours.

Denys Ovenden's meticulous paintings group plants and animals according to their natural habitats. Males, females, juveniles and seasonal and other variations are included where appropriate, and certain features of behaviour or the variations produced by zonation are illustrated in close-up or diagrammatic form.

The text concentrates on the natural history of the different inhabitants of the coast rather than on fine points of structure. John Barrett's immense experience brings a unique vividness to his account of the battle for survival in and beside the sea—and a wealth of fascinating detail. His explanations of the chemistry of seawater, the immensity of the seas, winds, tides, marine food chains, the effects of zonation and exposure on coastal wildlife, provide valuable background information on marine biology which will enhance any visit to the sea.

Also included are a table of windspeeds, a guide to harbour lights and signals and suggestions about making the most of time to look, enjoy and look again at the wonders and beauties of the coast.

Identification. First establish whereabouts you are: some creatures thrive on rocky but not on muddy shores. Refer to the contents page or flip through the page headings to find the correct habitat. Next, refer to the key on pp 4-9 where plants and animals are grouped in scientific order with diagrams and references to the main illustrations. The wonder and the beauty are available for all who look with patience and care—and a handlens.

A HANDGUIDE TO THE
SEA COAST

Painted by **Denys Ovenden**

Text by **John Barrett**

TREASURE PRESS

First published in Great Britain in 1981 by
William Collins Sons & Co Ltd
under the title
Collins Handguide to the Sea Coast

This edition published in 1987 by
Treasure Press
Michelin House
81 Fulham Road
London SW3 6RB

Reprinted 1988, 1989

ISBN 1 85051 116 0

Printed in Portugal by Oficinas Gráficas ASA

Contents

Pictorial Systematic Key   page 4

Introduction   10
  The immensity of the seas   11
  Seawater chemistry   12

The Open Sea: plankton   14
  Jellyfish   18
  Sharks and dolphins   20
The Open Coast: winter and breeding birds   22
Tides: rhythms, definitions and ranges   28
Waves: generation, power and progress   30
Rocky Shore: adaptations for survival;
  zonation   32
  very exposed: patterns and seals   38
  splash zone: shelter and exposure; plants and animals   40
  exposed: sloping, gully and pools   46
  sheltered: wrack/barnacle mosaics; pools; seaweeds   52
  crabs   60
  borers and builders   62
  oarweed (Laminaria) forest   64
  very sheltered: wracks   72
Sandy/muddy Shore: structure; burrowers, shells and worms   74
Strandline: shells and treasures   86
Sand-dunes and Shingle Banks: construction/destruction   88
Dunes: flowers, terns and jetsam   90
Shingle Banks: flowers and waders   94
Saltmarsh: construction/destruction; zonation; channels
  and pans   98
Estuaries: salinity and survival; fish, birds and eel-grass   106
Harbours: fishing quay; fish and piles   114
Table of Wind Speeds: Beaufort Scale   118
Harbour Lights, Flags and Hoots   119

Things to do   122

Books to read   124

Index   126

Pictorial Systematic Key

Nowhere in the world is there a greater variety of plants and animals as along the coasts generally and on the shore, between high and low tide, in particular. This Key is a shorthand summary of biological relationships and generalised shapes.

The largest subdivision of a Kingdom is the **PHYLUM** which comprises a number of CLASSES and their constituent **Orders**. Further refinement into the increasingly narrow definitions of Family, Genus and Species overcalls our space.

The measurements given in the captions to the illustrations in the body of the book refer to the dimension which commonsense would call the length of the organism. For those organisms which have no length as such, a bar against the outline shape in this Key indicates the dimension cited in the caption.

The numbers in this Key are page references to main textual information and illustrations of that group.

The plant kingdom

THALLOPHYTA: no differentation between root, stem & leaf.

ALGAE: contain chlorophyll (p.14); life usually includes sexual phase. All seaweeds are Algae. **56, 57**

Chlorophyceae (green seaweeds): contain chlorophyll only. **53, 57**

Phyaeophyceae (brown seaweeds): contain chlorophyll and brownish fucoxanthin. **34, 35, 47, 55, 57, 66, 67, 72, 73, 84, 85**

Diatoms are unicellular browns with a silica skeleton. **14, 15**

Rhodophyceae (red seaweeds): chlorophyll is masked by red pigment phycoerythin. **48, 49, 50, 54, 56, 57**

FUNGI: no chlorophyll; reproduction mainly by spores.

Lichenes (lichens): body of plant (thallus) composed of an association of fungal threads with an alga. **43**

PTERIDOPHYTA (ferns): root, stem & leaf differentiated; vascular system; reproduction alternation of spores & sexual stages. **45**

SPERMATOPHYTA: root, stem & leaf differentiated; seed bearing.

GYMNOSPERMAE (conifers): seeds in cones. Not in this book.

ANGIOSPERMAE (flowering plants): seeds in closed ovary (fruit). **44, 45, 91–105, 112, 113**

The animal kingdom

PROTOZOA: (single celled) **14–16**

PORIFERA (sponges): multicellular; usually encrusting; conspicuous exhalant holes (oscula) & many minute inhalant pores **48, 58, 85**

COELENTERATA: body consists of only two layers of cells between which is non-cellular jelly; food enters digestive cavity and waste leaves it through the one 'hole' which is in the middle of a flower-like 'polyp'.

HYDROZOA (hydroids, sea-firs): 'flower-heads' on communal 'stalks'. **51, 56, 85, 117**

SIPHONOPHORA (Portuguese Man-o'-War, By-the-Wind Sailor): hydrozoans specialised for floating, feeding, defending & reproducing welded into one complicated colony. **18**

SCYPHOZOA (jellyfish): life cycle includes a 'polyp' stage fixed to sea bottom. **18, 19**

Lucernaridia (stalked jellyfish): no free swimming stage. **113**

ANTHOZOA (sea-anemones, corals): no jellyfish stage; body cavity divided by vertical partitions. **51, 54, 81, 84, 85, 90, 116**

CTENOPHORA (comb-jellies): free swimming by 8 meridian lines of lashing threads ('cilia'). **51**

The evolution of a third layer of cells allowed ever more elaboration of organs and muscles.

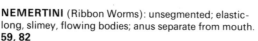

TURBELLARIA (Flat Worms): unsegmented; common mouth & anus; flowing movement. **108**

NEMERTINI (Ribbon Worms): unsegmented; elastic-long, slimey, flowing bodies; anus separate from mouth. **59, 82**

ANNELIDA (segmented or bristle worms): each segment of the ringed body contains repititions of most internal structures.

POLYCHAETA (marine worms): each segment with numerous bristles on each side.

Errant Worms move about freely. **59, 65, 82, 83, 109**

Sedentary Worms live in tubes. **59, 62, 82, 83**

ARTHROPODA far outnumber rest of Animal Kingdom put together. Jointed-legged; body encased in protective shell.

CRUSTACEA: body divided into head, thorax & abdomen; two pairs of antennae; many other appendages; respiration usually by gills. Mainly marine.

Cirripedia (barnacles): larvae confirm relationship; sessile. **36, 47, 108**

Malacostraca: head/thorax 8 segments, abdomen 6; thoracic & abdominal appendages distinct.

MYSIDACEA (opossum shrimps): thin shell fused with first 3 segments; thoracic appendages all divided into two. **51, 113**

ISOPODA (woodlouse-like): flattened from above downwards; inner antenna inconspicuous; eyes without stalks. **42, 108, 113, 117**

AMPHIPODA ('sandhoppers'): compressed sideways; rather curled; eyes not stalked. **55, 59, 87, 108, 117**

DECAPODA (shrimps, prawns, crabs, lobsters): eyes on moveable stalks; 5 pairs of 'walking' legs; head & thorax covered by shield (carapace); abdominal appendages carry 5 pairs feathery appendages; tail segment (telson) a broad fan. **50, 60, 61, 68, 69, 78, 79, 84, 85, 108**

INSECTA (insects): distinct head, thorax & abdomen; one pair of antennae; thorax with 3 pairs of legs.

Apterygota: wingless. **42, 54, 55**

Pterygota: nearly always winged. Essentially land-living. Some 2-winged flies lay eggs in rotting seaweed on strandline. Few small beetles live in this weed and on saltmarshes. Otherwise hardly a constituent of the marine fauna.

MOLLUSCA: unsegmented, soft bodied, usually protected by a limey shell secreted by a characteristic organ, the 'mantle'; all have a muscular 'foot'.

PLACOPHORA (chiton, coat-of-mail): symmetrical oval shell of 8 overlapping plates. **53**

GASTROPODA (slugs & snails): asymmetrical; always well developed foot; distinct with eyes & tentacles.

Prosobranchia (snails): twisted forms with well developed shell closed by leathery stopper (operculum); breathing by internal gills. **37, 42, 52, 53, 65–67, 78, 87, 108, 113**

Opisthobranchiata (slugs): shell reduced or absent; external gills. **51, 56, 66, 67, 78, 113**

Pulmonata: spiral shell; no operculum; respiration aerial; freshwater & terrestrial slugs & snails; not in this book.

CEPHALOPODA (octopus & cuttlefish): shell internal or absent; foot reduced to 8–10 arms with adhesive discs. **86, 112**

LAMELLIBRANCHIA (bivalves): shell with right & left valves usually enclosing all the soft parts; no head; foot laterally compressed; folded gills used for feeding as well as respiration. **63, 67, 75–81, 109**

BRYOZOA (POLYZOA) (sea-mats): encrusting colonies, each cell in the 'honeycomb' occupied by an individual animal of complicated structure. Each has a U-shaped gut with a mouth inside the circle of tentacles and the anus outside. **47, 64, 90**

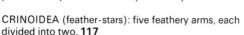

ECHINODERMATA (spiny-skinned): radially symmetrical; exoskeleton of calcareous plates; 'water-vascular system' which operates radial rows of protrusible hydraulic suckers (tube-feet).

CRINOIDEA (feather-stars): five feathery arms, each divided into two. **117**

ASTEROIDEA (starfish): usually 5, sometimes to 13, arms not sharply articulated to large body-disc. **66–69, 79**

OPHIUROIDEA (brittle-stars): clear demarkation between body-disc and the 5 arms which are at least five times longer than diameter of disc. **81, 84**

ECHINOIDEA (sea-urchins): globular or heart-shaped; spiney; bared test perforated by meridian lines of holes through which tube-feet protrude. **63, 65, 81, 116**

HOLOTHUROIDEA (sea-cucumbers): sausage-shaped, leathery body; mouth at one end surrounded by retractile tentacles. **112**

CHORDATA: possessing a cartilage rod (notochord) stiffening body length and a dorsal tubular nerve chord.

TUNICATA (sea-squirts): notochord only in larval stages; adults are sessile sacs with two siphons; body-wall of cellulose-like tunicin. **58, 116, 117**

CYCLOSTOMATA (lamprey & hagfish): body eel-like, cartilaginous skeleton; no scales or paired fins; sucking disc-mouth. **107**

VERTEBRATA: bilaterally symmetrical; adult notochord replaced by articulated skeleton.

Pisces (fish): two pairs of fins not of arm/leg type and other unpaired fins; gills at back of head.

ELASMOBRANCHII (skate, rays, sharks, dogfish): cartilaginous skeleton; mouth on underside of head; skin of small, tooth-like structures with sharp points; males have prominent copulatory organs (claspers) on inner side of pelvic fins. **20, 21, 85, 86, 115**

TELEOSTEI (typical fish): bony skeleton; usually with flat bony scales; mouth at point of head. **20, 66, 70, 71, 78, 79, 84, 85, 106, 107, 112, 115, 116**

Amphibia (frogs & newts): larval gills, adult lungs; moist, naked skin. All somewhat aquatic. Not in this book.

Reptilia: if present, 5-fingered limbs; dry skin covered by horny scales; no gills, cold blooded. **20**

Aves (birds): warm blooded but few dermal glands; feathers; horny scales on feet. **22–27, 90, 91, 95, 96, 110, 111, 114**

Mammalia: grow hair; secrete milk; warm blooded; body divided into two by diaphragm.

PINNEPEDIA (seals): 4 limbs with claws; brain large. **39, 90**

CETACEA (whales & porpoises): two paddle-limbs without claws; boneless fins; brain small. **20, 21**

PRIMATES (monkeys & man)

Introduction

What this book tries to do

This is a book about common 'things' that may be seen at the seaside. It is an outline natural history of the edge of the sea – of the water itself, the shores, sand, mud, shingle and rocky cliffs – and of the marvellously varied populations of plants and animals that live there. We hope the man often located on the Clapham omnibus and more generally in the street, but now on holiday with his family, will find in it a guide to wonders and beauties which he so far has not recognised because he does not quite know what to look for.

Denys Ovenden has been able to depict the various kinds of coast while including in his pictures plants and animals done so accurately, down to the number of ribs on a shell or rays in a fin or comparative lengths of successive appendages, that most of what anybody finds can be identified by careful comparison with his drawings. Of course, certainty will require confirmation from specialised texts (p.124).

We have had room to include only one portrait of each organism, though most might have appeared equally well in several pictures. By the same token, many creatures are not in a particular picture which might well belong there.

The captions to the drawings indicate the size range within which each organism is likely to occur. These are not absolute life limits; anything large started small. A line in the Key (pp.4–9) shows the dimensions used in the pictures.

Names are difficult: it is absurd not to use the vernacular, such as Sea Pink or Cod, where this exists. However, most seaweeds and marine animals have no vernacular name and it would have been senseless to invent one just for these pages; nobody else would know what we meant. So, where there is no alternative, we use the lingua franca of science.

A scientific name has two words. The second is the name of the species, conventionally never with a capital letter. The first is the name of the genus, always spelt with a capital, which links together closely related species. For those of us with even residual Latin and Greek, some of the names are descriptive. The rest of us, who grow buddleias, chrysanthemums and geraniums, have no need to flinch from *Idotea* or *Chondrus crispus*!

Given the necessary labels or names, we concentrate on the natural history of the organisms rather than on fine points of their structure. Living in and beside the sea is a dangerous business: the adaptations for survival are varied and wonderful, although some are also complicated and biologically difficult. This does not mean that they cannot be understood by anybody willing to take a little trouble to do so. We have done our best to use only simple words. No tool is required except a handlens. (Anybody who *ever* goes out without a handlens never sees very much.) The wonder and the beauty remain for all who look with patience and care.

The immensity of the seas

The planet Mercury has no water. On Venus the surface temperature of 471°C maintains vapour only. On Mars −43°C holds all water permanently frozen. Only on Earth have hundreds of millions of years' volcanic activity emitted vast volumes of water vapour. As Earth's surface cooled that vapour condensed to liquid. Only on Earth have movements in the global crust uplifted continents and depressed basins in which the great waters might collect.

The total world water supply is some 1,340 million cubic kilometres, of which 1,300 million are in the seas. A million years would pass before 10,000 pumps, each dealing with 450 million litres a day, had passed all the seawater once.

The conventional Northern hemisphere is 61% covered by seawater; the Southern 81%. A hemisphere centred just southeast of New Zealand is 90% sea; the complementary land hemisphere, with its centre in western France, is still just over half covered by water.

The depths below sea level are as irregular as the landward heights are above. The rivers draining off the land carry down a load of silt, sand and stones which build a 'continental shelf' sloping down to 200 m. The width of the shelf reflects the number and sizes of the local rivers and the hardness and angles of slope of the ground over which they run.

The seaward edge of the continental shelf abruptly steepens down the continental slope to 2,000 m. The floor of the oceans has wide plains, ridges and mountain peaks, some of which emerge at the surface as islands. The deepest submarine canyon is the 11,022 m in the Marianas Trench, southwest of Guam. Only 1% of the total ocean area is deeper than 6,000 m. 76% is between 6,000 and 3,000 and 7% between 3,000 and 200 m, leaving 16% covering the continental shelf. Even so, oceans are 5,000 times wider than they are deep. Within these great waters a chemical balance is maintained of beautiful and subtle complexity.

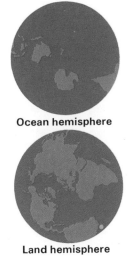

Ocean hemisphere

Land hemisphere

N.W. Atlantic continental shelf

Seawater chemistry and the secret of life

The complexity of the chemical balances within the 'dragon-green, the luminous, the dark, the serpent-haunted sea' and the layers of life that depend upon them lifts seawater into the shortest list of the natural wonders of the world.

Traces of every element in the periodic table can be detected. Molybdenum, titanium and strontium keep seaweeds healthy, whose structures may be based on silicon. Unless zinc, chromium and silver are in precise concentrations the tissues of most fish would be deformed. Sea-squirts need vanadium to be healthy.

If 100 tons of seawater are treated correctly, enough gold emerges to make a sovereign. The 13 million tons of silver held in solution are thousands of times more than man has ever mined.

Nearly all these elements are bonded with others into molecules which a chemist would call 'salts'. Phosphates, nitrates, bromides, carbonates and sulphates of sodium, magnesium and many other traces are part of the underpinning of life. If all 'salts' dissolved in seawater were extracted and dried, they would cover the continents in a layer 150 m deep. That would leave pure water still occupying 96.5% of the original volume.

99.9% of all the dissolved material derives from only 11 elements. Of this mass 75% is common salt – sodium chloride. 1,000 gm of seawater normally contains 34–36 gm of 'solids': that is its 'salinity'. Icemelt in summer causes local polar dilutions. River flow lowers the eastern Baltic to 5 parts per 1,000. Low rain and fierce evaporation raise Red Sea salinity

---

Concentration of some elements in seawater

parts per million		parts per 1000 million	
chlorine	18980	arsenic	10–20
sodium	10561	iron	20
magnesium	1272	manganese	10
sulphur	884	copper	10
calcium	400	zinc	5
potassium	380	lead	4
bromine	65	selenium	4
carbon	28	caesium	2
strontium	13	uranium	1.5
boron	4.6	molybdenum	0.5
silicon	4	thorium	0.5
fluorine	1.4	cercium	0.4
nitrogen	0.7	silver	0.3
aluminium	0.5	vanadium	0.3
rubidium	0.2	lanthanum	0.3
lithium	0.1	yttrium	0.3
barium	0.05	nickel	0.1
iodine	0.05	scandium	0.04
		mercury	0.003
		gold	0.006
		radium	0.0000002

to 40 ppt and the landlocked Dead Sea to over 200. On the acidity (pH) scale where less than 7 counts as acid and more than 7 is alkaline, seawater ranges between 8.0 and 8.4.

Without oxygen life is impossible, in the sea as on land. The waters hold oxygen in solution abundantly, most of all at the edge of the sea where waves and gales mix air and water. Inhaling oxygen is inevitably followed by exhaling carbon dioxide. This CO_2 is necessary for the growth and reproduction of plants, powered by the energy of the sun (photosynthesis, p.14). The circulation of carbon in the sea is close to the secret of life.

Nobody has succeeded in making from its constituent parts a 'seawater' in which plants and animals will flourish. Most die quickly in it. The secret is beautifully mysterious: the man-made mixture lacks 'life' and nobody knows how to supply it. What man destroys he cannot recreate.

The same amount of heat raises the temperature of 1 cu.m. of water or 3,000 cu.m. of air by 1°C: seawater temperatures change more slowly than the air's. The British west coast maximum of $c.17°C$ and the North Sea's 15°C are reached in September and the normal minima of 8°C and 4°C in February (in contrast to 30°C to −10°C on land). Changes of temperature in the surface layers are conducted downwards so slowly that at about 100 m the water is warmest in winter and coldest in summer. Down at 200 m temperature does not change at all.

The penetration of light is restricted by the sand, silt and other solids held in suspension. 'Turbidity', measured in parts per million, varies from $c.$ 5 ppm of west coasts through to 1,000 ppm in the North Sea, 6,000 ppm in big estuaries and 50,000 ppm in the winter Thames. Only 1% of the surface light or energy at midday survives at 100 m and so little at 200 m that no plants can grow there.

In still water suspended solids sink at different rates

	max. diam. in mm	settling velocity in cm/sec in water at 20°C
coarse sand	2.0	347
fine sand	0.2	3.47
silt	0.02	0.0347
clay	0.002	0.00347

Mud (silt/clay) accumulates in estuaries because waves seldom inhibit vertical settlement (p.98).

The chemicals in seawater, essential for life, tend to sink into the deeps: but life can hardly exist down where sunlight does not penetrate. So life depends upon vertical mixing of the waters.

The waters of great ocean surface currents, e.g. the Gulf Stream, driven from the equator by the Trade Winds and deflected into high latitudes by the rotation of the earth, cool and sink. Counter-moving deep cold currents are thus established which move back towards the equator. In areas where the continental shelf shallows gently, the momentum upwards of the cold current, laden with nutrients, carries it to the surface. These upwellings enrich the surface waters, stimulate plankton production and multiply the food chains.

The Open Sea: Plankton

Just drifting or, at best, feebly pulsing in the surface layers of the sea are living things in numbers that far exceed flakes of snow or hailstones in a squall. They constitute the plankton (Gk. for 'drifting feebly').

Only those plants containing chlorophyll can use the energy of sunlight to build carbohydrates which are then converted into complicated proteins by suitable combinations with phosphorus, sulphur and nitrogen. Chlorophyll is a unique mixture of green and yellow pigments and is itself not changed during food manufacture. It acts as a catalyst to allow protein building to continue as long as the quality of the light is good enough. This 'photosynthesis' comes close to the origin of life and still sustains it worldwide.

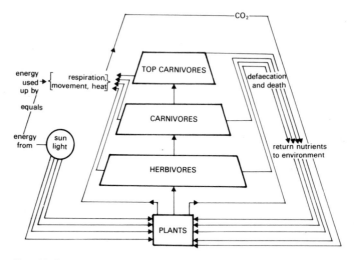

Pyramid of numbers: energy and the cycling of nutrients support successive consumer levels, in the plankton as elsewhere.

These microscopic, single-celled plants containing chlorophyll constitute the base of marine life. Their elaborate molecules are the essential food of animals which browse on them. These herbivores are then eaten by carnivores and they by top-carnivores. Energy is transferred along the links of food chains – 'all flesh is grass'.

Diatoms and dinoflagellates
Plankton plants are single-celled, green or brown **diatoms**. They have a silicate skeleton of two halves fitting together like an old-fashioned pill box which may be strung together in chains.

Dinoflagellates are a second constituent of the plankton. They have a plant's cellulose cell walls and an animal's power of movement, lashing two whiplike threads. Some photosynthesise; others eat smaller organisms. Some feed in the dark and fix energy by day.

Between five and sixty species of diatom and dinoflagellates may occur in a litre of seawater. Most are less than 0.01 mm across. Being invisible, the numbers are difficult to imagine: 20,000 of the largest and ten million of the smaller in a bucketful of seawater; a thousand in a thimbleful of the Baltic. The plankton drifting under a hectare of coastal water weighs more than a hectare of fully grown potatoes. All depend on the chemical nutrients in seawater.

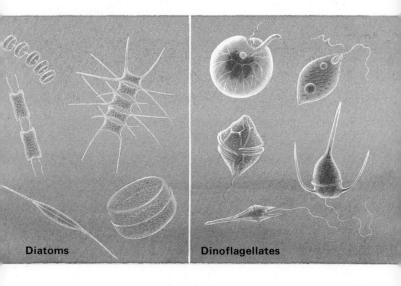

Diatoms

Dinoflagellates

One-celled animals, Protozoans, browse these sea-meadows. Lashing **Ciliates** progress at 1 mm/sec. **Foraminifera** capture food through holes in their shells of calcium carbonate. **Radiolaria** have shells of silicon and strontium sulphate. So vast and ancient is the number of Protozoans that their skeletons constitute a muddy ooze on ocean floors that deepens a few centimetres each thousand years and is now hundreds of metres thick.

The numbers and varieties of organisms recognisably 'animal' living in the plankton throughout their lives are commensurate with the plants. Most are tiny crustaceans, untold millions of millions eaten by fish; also minute jellyfish, worms, sea-squirts and delicate molluscs. Many adults whose movements are not at the mercy of currents and so are not counted as plankton – fish, crabs, oysters, barnacles, worms, etc – have egg and larval stages which are planktonic. At each laying a cod releases a million and a half eggs. In the southern North Sea six million million plaice eggs are produced annually.

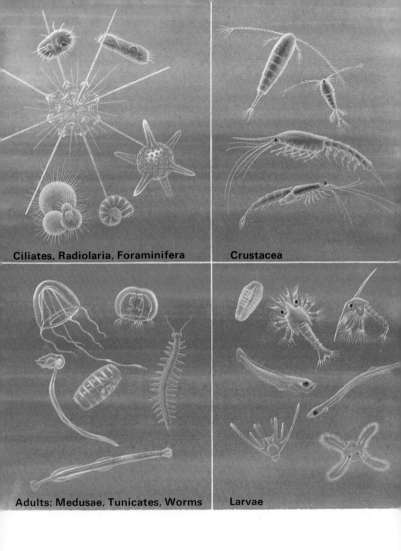

Ciliates, Radiolaria, Foraminifera

Crustacea

Adults: Medusae, Tunicates, Worms

Larvae

All mussels in a bed spawn simultaneously, to increase the chance that sperm meets egg. Each female ejects 25 million eggs and each male many more sperms. So much passes into the food chains that a day later only 150,000 fertilised eggs survive above each square metre of musselbed. Of those, not more than ten eventually settle as adults.

Meanwhile each adult mussel eats daily 100,000 larvae and untold diatoms from the 45 litres it filters. Sixty tonnes of mussel weight develop per hectare per year and all from plankton.

The Open Sea: Plankton

A Blue Whale, 8 m long and 15 tonnes at birth, increases by 500 kg per week, all from mother's milk. She lives only by sieving plankton. Two years later that calf will weigh 75 tonnes – all from plankton. A man swallows at least a thousand living things in a mouthful of seawater.

At each link along a foodchain only some 10–15% of what is eaten is converted into bodyweight. The rest supplies energy for movement, metabolism, reproduction, respiration and so on. The biological balances depend upon the chemical: each is like a stupendous house of cards. Man's activities now threaten the stability of these delicate structures.

By the time the Gulf Stream reaches our coasts the nutrient salts that support the plant plankton are diluted. However, they are so enriched by nutrients in river-water draining off the Continent that, particularly in the Channel, Irish Sea and round Scotland, the plankton multiplies and floating food is again available, notably for smaller fish which support so many seabird colonies.

Ocean currents and plankton density in the N.E. Atlantic. The paler the 'water' the greater the density.

The Open Sea: Jellyfish

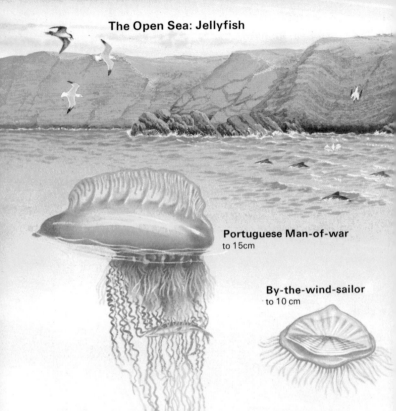

Portuguese Man-of-war
to 15cm

By-the-wind-sailor
to 10 cm

Jellyfish drift worldwide in the plankton, pulsing rhythmically. Very simple animals, their bulk is non-living jelly; the outside of the umbrella is secured by one layer of cells while the only other layer is a digesting lining to the gut cavity. The mouth lobes are elaborated from this, with stinging cells to narcotise struggling food. Commonest in late summer; erratic in numbers; mass strandings may be of post-breeding adults. *Aurelia* abounds from the Arctic to the Equator; the phosphorescent *Pelagia* is western; *Rhizostoma*, *Cyanea* and *Chrysaora* more southern.

The **Portuguese Man-of-war** and **By-the-wind-sailor** are technically not jellyfish but a complex aggregate of individual polyps, each with a special function – reproduction, digestion, defence. The highly contractile tentacles of the Man-of-war deliver a burning sting. Persistent southwest winds blowing against its gas-filled bag, which flops this way and that to keep wet and pliable, and against the By-the-wind-sailor's horny sail, bring them to our shores from the tropics. The last large arrival was in 1954.

In the distance plankton feeds sand-eels; sand-eels feed kittiwakes and the skuas who rob them, and mackerel; mackerel feed gannets, porpoises and men. The plankton is the first link in every marine foodchain.

Aurelia aurita
7–30 cm

Chrysaora isosceles
10–40 cm

Pelagia noctiluca
7–15 cm

Cyanea lamarki
7–30 cm

Rhizostoma pulmo
to 60 cm

19

The Open Sea: Sharks and Dolphins

The **Loggerhead** is one of three turtles (the others are the Leathery and Kemp's Ridley) which, when young, may be swept out of the Caribbean by hurricanes. Without landmarks, they drift northeast on the Gulf Stream for over a year. Food – crabs, jellyfish, clams – is almost nonexistent. Temperatures fall ever lower. Few survivors reach our waters.

The massive, scaleless **Sunfish** feeds on plankton and small fish. Cold reduces to torpidity those that drift to us from southern water. The even more massive, but cold water, **Basking Shark** feeds only on plankton. Swimming at 2 knots, it filters some 1,500 tonnes of water per hour. Not uncommon in summer, near the surface. Its survival is endangered by overfishing for its liver, yielding 600 kg of oil. Gestation $3\frac{1}{2}$ years.

The **Blue Shark** and **Tope** eat fish. Their meat is fit only for bait. Both are victims of commercial 'sport'.

Porpoise and **dolphins** are all warm-blooded mammals adapted for life at sea by having no hind limbs or hair, with transverse tail flukes, a blowhole in the top of their head. They mate and give birth at sea. Like seals, they can dive for unexpectedly long periods because the urge to inhale is not triggered until the concentration of carbon dioxide in the brain has long exceeded a level that would cause a feeling of suffocation in land mammals.

They have a gestation period of 11–13 months, reach maturity at about 12 years and live for 30. They eat fish, crustacea and cuttlefish and may be eaten by Killer Whales and sharks. Only the porpoise does not leap out of the water. Some Bottle-nosed have 'enjoyed' friendly relations with swimmers.

Loggerhead Turtle
150–180 cm

Sunfish
to 3 m, 1400 kg

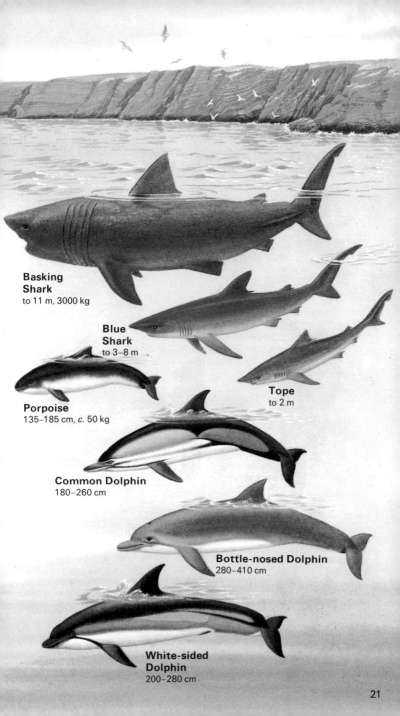

Basking Shark
to 11 m, 3000 kg

Blue Shark
to 3–8 m

Porpoise
135–185 cm, *c.* 50 kg

Tope
to 2 m

Common Dolphin
180–260 cm

Bottle-nosed Dolphin
280–410 cm

White-sided Dolphin
200–280 cm

21

Glaucous Gull
l. 70, s. 135 cm

Great Black-back Gull
l. 74, s. 165 cm

Peregrine
l. 38–48, s. 68–78 cm

Common Scoter
l. 48, s. 55 cm

Velvet Scoter
l. 56, s. 65 cm

Long-tailed Duck
l. ♂ 53, ♀ 41, s. 50–55 cm

Eider
l. 58, s. 65 cm

The Arctic is a source of life beyond imagining, greatly influencing the annual turning of our coastal year. Summer days, pulsing jellyfish, clamorous bird cliffs and flowers inevitably turn to seer winter when **Long-tailed Ducks** and strange **gulls**, including a few pale grey **Glaucous**, come from Iceland and Arctic Russia to our northern shores. **Common Scoter** that nested by Highland lakes are joined by refugees from Arctic cold on the open sea off eastern and southern coasts. **Velvets** flee the Baltic. Northern **Eider** join ours as they move south from the north and west of Scotland where they nest abundantly and 'receive their ancient state and instinct with the sea'. Winter 'matters' on the coast just as much as summer.

''Vainly the sharp and hard points of the marram grasses drew their circles on the sand: the Icicle Spirit was coming . . . As Tarka and his mate were running down to meet the flood tide in the pill, a baying broke out in the sky . . . The long skein of south-wending geese swung round in the wind . . .''
Tarka the Otter, Henry Williamson, The Bodley Head.

Red-throated Diver
l. 53–58, s. 63 cm

Great Northern Diver
l. 68–71, s. 80 cm

In October, when ice relocks the Arctic, 'black' geese move south. Most pale-breasted Brents go to America; a few from Novaya Zemlya and Greenland turn to Scotland and Ireland, while their dark Siberian relations winter off our east and south coasts, on quiet, wide flats, upending among wigeon and other ducks for eel-grass (p.112) and wracks (p.34) until high tide drives them onto landward grass. Short, noisy, guttural clankings call nervous warning of intrusion.

Barnacles from Greenland and Spitzbergen winter on solitary coastal marshes in the Hebrides, Solway and Ireland, gabbling small-terrier-barkings chorus when they fly. The music of the spheres sounds as geese flight against a February dawn.

Most **Great Northern Divers** nest in Arctic America. A few from Greenland and Iceland winter on our open coasts. So do **Red-throateds**. Their circumpolar nesting has a southern extension to northwest Scotland.

light

dark

Brent Geese
l. 56–61, s. 75–85 cm

Barnacle Goose
l. 58–69, s. 95 cm

23

Coastal Birds: Breeding

Herring Gull
l. 60, s. 130 cm

Lesser Black-back Gull
l. 55, s. 125 cm

Herring Gull imm.
l. 56, s. 130 cm

Great Black-back Gull imm.
l. 70, s. 165 cm

Puffin
l. 30, s. 45 cm

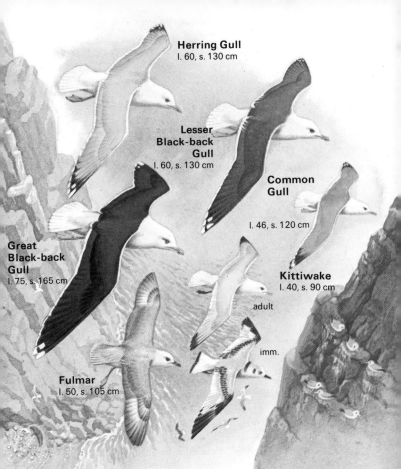

Herring Gull
l. 60, s. 130 cm

Lesser Black-back Gull
l. 60, s. 130 cm

Common Gull
l. 46, s. 120 cm

Great Black-back Gull
l. 75, s. 165 cm

Kittiwake
l. 40, s. 90 cm

adult

imm.

Fulmar
l. 50, s. 105 cm

Britain and Ireland provide the most important breeding places for sea-birds in the northeast Atlantic. The populations of these four **gulls** are all on the increase, the Herring Gull's most of all. Ever more these follow the plough and infest rubbish tips.

The **Kittiwake** is also on the increase. It is wholly marine, although restricted to cliffs, many on remote islands. In winter they spread out over the oceans, plunge-diving for small fish.

The **Fulmar** continues to increase dramatically as new colonies start ever further south from their origin in Iceland. In winter they range the open sea north to the edge of the ice, scavenging round fishing boats and picking larger planktonic animals.

Rats, gull predation and erosion of habitat are all possible causes of **Puffins'** decline, as are oil, chemical and effluent pollution. Perhaps, too, over-fishing has so much disturbed the marine biological balances that their food is made scarce thereby.

Puffin
l. 30, s. 45 cm

Rock Dove
l. 33, s. 52 cm

Black Guillemot
l. 35, s. 36 cm

Tree Mallow
to 1 m

bridled

Guillemot
l. 42, s. 105 cm

Little Auk
l. 20, s. 30 cm

Guillemot and **Razorbill** are decreasing. In winter both spread over coastal waters, the razorbills more to the south. They dive mostly for sand-eels and sprats. The 'spectacles' of bridled guillemots occur on less than 1% in the south to 70% in Iceland.

When adults are startled off their breeding ledges, the single eggs would crash to destruction were they not so pear-shaped that they spin round on their narrow end. The nests of circumpolar **Black Guillemots**, from which few travel far even in winter, are all north and/or west of Anglesey. Straggling Arctic-breeding **Little Auks** occur only in winter.

Shags nest on exposed rocky cliffs, particularly north and west, in increasing numbers. They dive mainly for sand-eels, sprats and pollack. They travel little in winter.

Ravens are widespread and **Jackdaws** increasingly common cliff-nesters. **Crows** are common too, Hooded replacing Carrion in the Isle of Man, Ireland and northwest Scotland. **Choughs**, common round the coasts 200 years ago, disappeared from England in 1968, leaving 100 pairs between Pembrokeshire, N. Wales, Isle of Man and the Western Isles and 600 in Ireland. Why they became so few is a mystery.

Jackdaw
l. 33, s. 50 cm

Crow
l. 47, s. 70 cm

Hooded Crow
l. 47, s. 70 cm

Raven
l. 64, s. 85 cm

Chough
l. 40, s. 60 cm

Razorbill
l. 42, s. 66 cm

imm.

Shag
l. 90, s. 150 cm

ad.

27

The Tides

The tidal rhythms in offshore waters are less obvious than along the shore where they partly control the distribution of plants and animals by exposing them at different levels to different degrees of danger from drying out (p.32).

High tide never reaches the same level on the shore on two consecutive days. On each of the first seven during a 28-day period, high tide comes higher and higher up the beach and, at the 6-hour interval, low tide sinks lower and lower down. Then, during the second seven days, high tide is less and less high, while low tide gets correspondingly less low; i.e. the vertical 'range' contracts to a minimum. During the third seven days, high tide progresses upwards again and low tide downwards, to the second maximum range. In the fourth period, the range diminishes to a second minimum. The 28-day rhythm then goes round again.

The two maxima are the 'spring' tides, associated with the full and new moon, and the two minima are the 'neaps' at half waxing and waning moon. All tides oscillate about a line halfway down the shore – 'mean sea level', MSL.

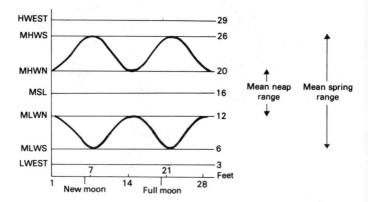

Heights daily of high and low water during a typical 28-day period where the mean spring range is 20 ft and the neap range 8 ft. The same generalised shape applies to almost any place on the British coast.

Month by month from December, the spring range increases to a maximum in March from which it declines to a minimum in June (while still the biggest tide in that 28-day period). Then it opens to a second maximum in September and down to a second minimum in December.

The March and September extreme high water (HWEST) and extreme low water (LWEST) occur near the equinox and so are the 'equinoctial spring tides' – the biggest, high and low, tides of the year. Likewise the seasonal range of neaps will vary above and below the mean (MHWN, MLWN).

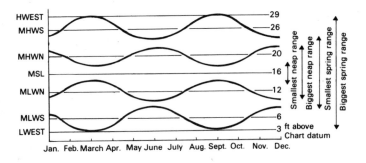

Generalised curves to show the variations month by month throughout a year of the range of spring and neap tides, where the mean spring range is 20 ft and the mean neap range 8 ft. The same shapes would apply at places where the ranges are different.

Long lengths of coast have a 3–5 m spring range. Where water is squeezed into the funnel of the Bristol Channel, the range at Chepstow and Avonmouth is some 12 m. In southwest Scotland chance shapes of geography reduce the range to 1 m. At any one place all spring highs occur at about the same time of day and the lows necessarily six hours later. The clock-hour differs from place to place as the tidal rhythms progress round the coast.

Around springs today's high water may be only 20 minutes later than yesterday's: around neaps, 80 minutes. Hence the 50-minute average so commonly cited and so misleading in the short run. Computing expertise enables the Institute of Oceanographic Sciences to publish Tide Tables for all major ports from which local lists are derived. The local times are available from coastguards and often even on tiny quay notice boards.

Tide is essentially a vertical movement which necessarily has a horizontal component flowing all round the coasts, six hours this way and six hours that. At neaps 1–2 knots, but at springs, particularly where the equinoctials are compressed into narrows (notably the Pentland Firth) the tide runs at 8 knots or more. Solid particles held in suspension in water moving so fast constantly sandpaper the rocks, so inhibiting some settlement on them from the plankton at the delicate moment of adult attachment to the shore.

Waves

Waves are generated by wind: no wind, no waves. The faster the wind, the longer time and distance across the sea it blows, the larger the waves. Approximately

wave speed = $\frac{3}{4}$ wind speed (p.118)

wave height in metres (crest to trough) =

$$\frac{(\text{wind speed in knots})^2}{12}$$

In theory wave speed could equal wind speed, but the wind never blows steadily and long enough for this to happen. Wind directions change as centres of low pressure pass by; tomorrow's wind is likely to beat down waves generated by today's.

Gales caused by steep but slow-moving pressure gradients may intensify during a second and, rarely, a third day. Then mounding corrugations of water, 10 metres from trough to crest, drive coastward until the friction caused by shallowing slows down the foot while the wind still forces forward the back until a vertical or even over-the-vertical wall of water smashes onto the rocks at 100 kph.

The tumultuous sucking, swashing, thumping of 150 tonnes per metre per wave threatens all shore life with physical destruction. 120 tonne concrete pyramids placed to protect the seaward foundation were flipped over Plymouth breakwater by a later gale. In 1877 3,000 tonnes of Wick harbour wall were pushed back in one piece. Boulders are lifted and smashed together. Cliffs are undercut and collapse. Pockets of air trapped in the waves are forced into cracks under pressure with the potential of high explosive, throwing tonnes of spray high over the cliffs. Yet, in the calm of next day, all who live on the shore are quietly about their business.

The wave-trains, no longer breaking, persist as a diminishing ground swell until a new wind drives steepening waves before a new gale. At neap tides, the lowest levels of the shore remain covered and the highest will receive only lashing spray. On exposed coasts, however, the middle

shore is assaulted by every gale as the tide rises over it and again as it ebbs down. Meanwhile another shore, protected by headlands, with its back to the prevailing wind, is hardly ever open to damage by waves.

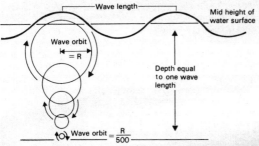

Wave length

Mid height of water surface

Wave orbit = R

Depth equal to one wave length

Wave orbit = $\frac{R}{500}$

Watch flotsam: wave motion progresses but not the water. At a depth equal to the wavelength, the radius of the drops' circular movement is less than 1/500 of what it is on the surface. Creatures in shallow water live almost undisturbed by waves.

Rocky Shores: adaptation

Plants and animals living on rocky shores have to be adapted to cope not only with tides and waves but also to varying hardnesses and textures of the rock and the angle and exposure of the slope to sunshine. The temperature of the water, its turbidity, salinity and man's toxic effluents are all powerful controls.

No wonder that populations vary enormously from shore to shore. Except on those few where waves are larger than tides, most organisms live in horizontal bands, or 'zones', along rocky shores, too simply if conveniently referred to as 'tidal' zones. Closely related species often live in vertical series (pp.34, 36).

To absorb nutrients seaweeds have to be submerged: but to photosynthesis (p.14) they need light. The quantity of light diminishes with depth. The optimum compromise would be at mean sea level, but that is where mechanical damage by wave action is most likely.

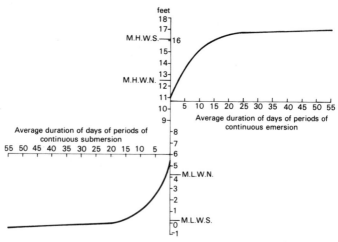

The ecology of Rocky Shores (J. R. Lewis)
Hodder & Stoughton

Most animals breathe oxygen held in solution in seawater. To dry out is a mortal danger. Survival over low tide may lie under damp seaweeds, but on a shore sheltered from almost all wave action the seaweeds may be so abundant that some animals would be smothered. On the other hand, as exposure increases, the seaweeds become smashed by waves beyond the point of being able to provide cover for animal survival.

Other adaptations to resist desiccation succeed as long as the rock surface is shaded from the midday sun, although the heat may be reduced sufficiently when spring high tides are in the middle of the day. Then again, body-water may freeze when uncovered by deep winter low tides.

Access to light, waterborne oxygen and food, desiccation, overheating and supercooling are all overlain by the tidal rhythms in such complex variety that no short length of rocky shore has a natural history precisely the same as the next. Zonation, however, is a feature common to all.

A general pattern summarises this immense complexity. All organisms that cannot survive any exposure to air must live below low water of equinoctial springs (LWEST). Equinoctial highs (HWEST) limit upwards those that must be soaked occasionally and do not survive in only the chance of spray. The lowest high water limits those that must be covered twice a day. Those that must spend even a few minutes each day out of the sea cannot live lower than the highest low tide level.

The pattern devised by Professor and Mrs Stevenson has worldwide application.

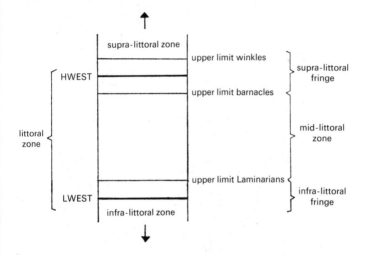

The supra-littoral fringe is out of reach of all but the highest tide and spray; it may be quite dry for two or more weeks together. The mid-littoral is covered and uncovered by almost every tide of the year. The infra-littoral fringe is exposed only at the lowest springs and even then hardly has time to dry out.

Zonation is hard to detect on sandy or muddy shores because distributions there are controlled by the size of the particles of the ground into which animals burrow and much less by the tides.

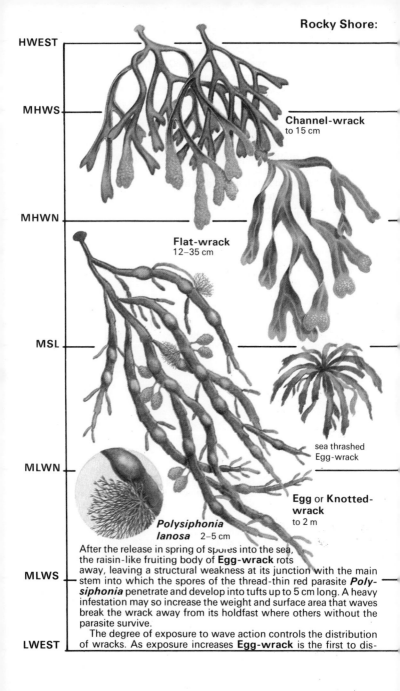

HWEST

MHWS

Channel-wrack
to 15 cm

MHWN

Flat-wrack
12–35 cm

MSL

sea thrashed
Egg-wrack

MLWN

Egg or **Knotted-
wrack**
to 2 m

*Polysiphonia
lanosa* 2–5 cm

After the release in spring of spores into the sea, the raisin-like fruiting body of **Egg-wrack** rots away, leaving a structural weakness at its junction with the main stem into which the spores of the thread-thin red parasite **Poly-siphonia** penetrate and develop into tufts up to 5 cm long. A heavy infestation may so increase the weight and surface area that waves break the wrack away from its holdfast where others without the parasite survive.

MLWS

LWEST

The degree of exposure to wave action controls the distribution of wracks. As exposure increases **Egg-wrack** is the first to dis-

Zonation and Exposure

appear, then **Flat-wrack**. The others survive moderate battering but none can live in extreme exposure. Despite thickened cell walls, **Channel** and Flat-wrack lose 90% of tissue water during neap drying. During the short immersion, necessarily always in shallow water, they assimilate nutrients with unusual rapidity. Where **Egg** and **Bladder-wrack** have gas-filled bladders to float fronds up towards the light, the lower **Saw-wrack**'s bushy growth develops a larger surface receptive to fainter light. **F. ceranoides** and **F. vesiculosus** var. **vadorum** are confined to estuaries.

Limpets, winkles and topshells eat most sporelings which settle quickly from 1 million wrack eggs per plant released annually into the plankton. Survivors live 3–4 years. Egg wrack to 15.

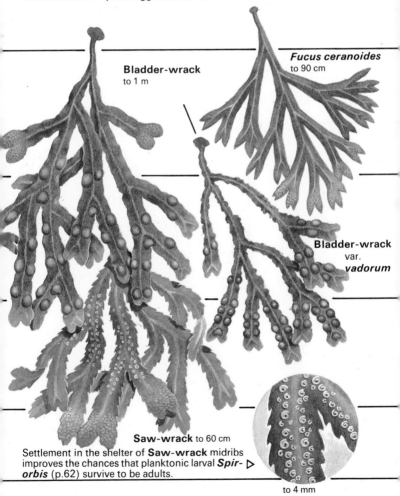

Bladder-wrack
to 1 m

Fucus ceranoides
to 90 cm

Bladder-wrack
var.
vadorum

Saw-wrack to 60 cm

Settlement in the shelter of **Saw-wrack** midribs improves the chances that planktonic larval *Spir-* ▷
orbis (p.62) survive to be adults.

to 4 mm

35

Rocky Shore: Barnacles, Winkles and Topshells

Barnacles are crustaceans, related to crabs and shrimps. Fertilised eggs released into the sea initiate planktonic larval stages. The zone of adult settlement on the rocks is controlled by chemical attraction of the larvae to their own species, so maintaining the density of population which may be 100,000 per sq. m. of rock surface.

The movement of large wracks brushes off the barnacle larvae at the critical moment of settlement. So barnacles are scarce where wracks abound and become commoner as increasing exposure prevents wrack survival. They are abundant in the midshore zone over which the waves pass four times every day, laden with oxygen and planktonic food which the barnacles, having slid open their central plates, draw in on a current established by rhythmical kicking of their 'legs'.

The warm water **Chthamalus** and **Balanus perforatus** are at their northern limits in southwest Britain, where cold water **B. balanoides** is towards its southern. The four-plated Australian **Elminius** arrived in the Channel by 1945 and spreads steadily northwards.

Dogwhelks and blennies eat barnacles.

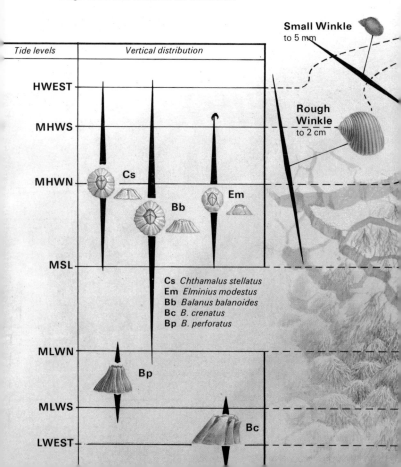

Small Winkle
to 5 mm

Rough Winkle
to 2 cm

Tide levels	Vertical distribution
HWEST	
MHWS	
MHWN	Cs
	Bb
	Em
MSL	
MLWN	Bp
MLWS	
LWEST	Bc

Cs *Chthamalus stellatus*
Em *Elminius modestus*
Bb *Balanus balanoides*
Bc *B. crenatus*
Bp *B. perforatus*

Winkles fertilise eggs by copulation. Topshells depend upon chance meeting of sperms and eggs released into the sea. The central column within a winkle's shell is solid; within a topshell, hollow.

They all ingest fragments rasped off seaweeds by the hard teeth on the underside of their horny ribbon-tongues.

Recent work proves that the name **Rough Winkle** covers an aggregate of four separate species which differ considerably, amongst other things, in the size and shape of the penis. Between them they occur through a large vertical zone and range of exposure.

The **Small Winkle** flourishes in exposure whereas, because of their shape and the abundance of seaweed food, the other winkles and topshells are much commoner on more sheltered shores.

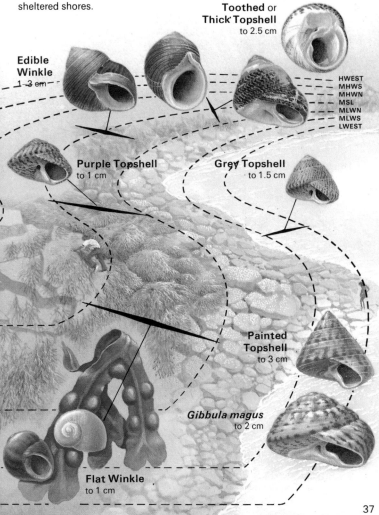

Toothed or
Thick Topshell
to 2.5 cm

**Edible
Winkle**
1-3 cm

HWEST
MHWS
MHWN
MSL
MLWN
MLWS
LWEST

Purple Topshell
to 1 cm

Grey Topshell
to 1.5 cm

**Painted
Topshell**
to 3 cm

Gibbula magus
to 2 cm

Flat Winkle
to 1 cm

Rocky Shore: Exposed Patterns

A wide zone of barnacle/mussel competition dominates shores that are not too steep but are exposed to surf. Mussels are generally lower than barnacles but sometimes they are so dense to above MSL that no barnacles survive. Sometimes mussels are in discreet patches amongst the barnacles around MLWN.

Mussel larvae are drawn by chemical attraction to settle by or on adults. They extrude sticky elastic threads giving anchorage like tent guys to the front half of the shell, allowing the back to flex with changing angles of water thrusts.

Eventually those die at the base of the growing mussel lump, smothered by later settlers, and all are swept away. The cleared area will then be occupied by barnacle larvae. Elsewhere mussel settlement in dead barnacles inhibits further barnacle attachment and another lump of mussels builds and dies.

Little else survives along these shores except tiny tufts of a few red seaweeds, remnants of black lichen and an occasional small limpet.

Evolution of the isolated **Grey Atlantic Seal** populations in the Baltic, northeast Atlantic and Canada is producing separate species. Some 95% of the NE Atlantic and 75% of the world total live round Britain – in Scotland, the Farne Islands, Pembrokeshire and Ireland.

In autumn the females come ashore to caves, remote beaches and onto small islands to drop a single pup, 80 cm long, weighing 14 kg. Each male protects a harem of 5–10 females. After three weeks' suckling, females desert the pup which now weighs 43 kg – those less than 40 kg do not survive the winter. Mature in six years, females exceed 2 m and 80 kg, with males larger. Copulation follows suckling but the development of the foetus is delayed until February.

Seals have separate hauling-out sites for moulting and for use while fishing. They eat crustaceans, octopus and squid as well as many fish, including cod, salmon, and sand-eels, but nobody knows in what proportions. Nobody knows nearer than 50% either way how many seals there are, but populations increase.

A diving seal exhales air to reduce buoyancy; its heartbeat falls from 150 to 10 per minute, so conserving oxygen stored copiously in blood and muscles. The normal fishing dive lasts 5–7 minutes but can be 20. Like dolphins, the carbon dioxide concentration in the brain that triggers the next breath is much higher than in land mammals. Breaking surface, the heart revs up from 10 to 150 and a few deep breaths wash out the carbon dioxide.

Grey Seal
2–3 m

Rocky Shore: Exposure and Shelter

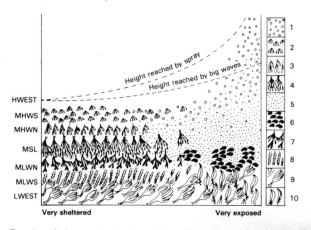

Zonation of plants and animals on shores of varying exposure. **1**, Small Winkles. **2**, Channel-wrack. **3**, Spiral-wrack. **4**, Egg-wrack. **5**, Barnacles. **6**, Mussels. **7**, Bladder-wrack. **8**, Saw-wrack. **9**, Oarweed. **10**, *Alaria esculenta*.

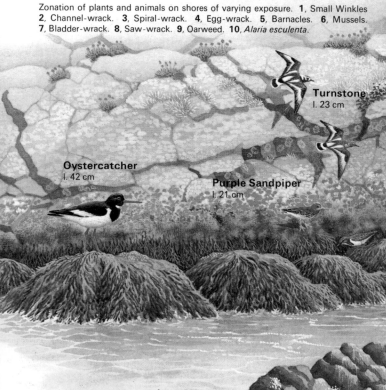

The natural history differs greatly within a few yards when the slope of the cliffs and their attitude to wind and waves change abruptly.

Rock Pipits breed along the tall, steep, exposed splash zone which is dominated by lichens and where no seaweeds survive. Round the corner, sheltered from the worst of the waves, Sea Pinks, Red Fescue etc. (p.44) grow in the truncated splash zone only a few feet above the Channel-wrack in which **Turnstone**, **Purple Sandpipers** and **Oystercatchers** can always find food.

Rock Pipit
l.16 cm

41

Rocky Shore: Splash Zone – animals and lichens

Progression upwards through the splash zone is an evolutionary route from the sea onto the land, particularly for animals without planktonic larval stages. However, few species survive the waterless weeks that characterise these levels.

Sea-slaters and **Bristle-tails** are nocturnal scavengers, emerging in their thousands from damp cracks.

The eggs of some **Rough Winkles** hatch at the level where the adults live. Gills show evolution towards being lungs. While marine creatures normally excrete ammonium which is poisonous unless immediately diluted by the sea, Rough and **Small Winkles** excrete the less toxic urea, as do land animals.

Although zoned higher than the Rough, the Small Winkle is losing the evolutionary race onto land because its larval development is still in the plankton. The fertilised eggs are released only at spring tides in winter when gales are most likely to splash them down into the sea. The final change (metamorphosis) leaves the tiny adults low on the shore, where, when covered by seawater they move upwards; when becoming uncovered by the ebb tide they retreat into dark cracks. The combination brings them at last into the splash zone where Rock Pipits eat them.

Rough Winkles are many colours. As exposure increases progressively deeper grooves between the whorls structurally strengthen the shells. Small Winkles survive by living in deep cracks.

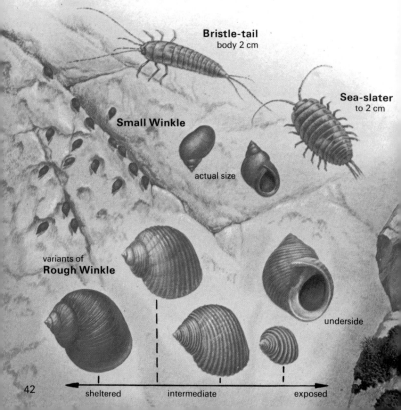

Bristle-tail
body 2 cm

Sea-slater
to 2 cm

Small Winkle

actual size

variants of
Rough Winkle

underside

sheltered   intermediate   exposed

Lichens. An alga, either single-celled or a full-scale seaweed, uses the sun's energy to make carbohydrates from water and carbon dioxide (photosynthesis, p.14). Unable to do this, a fungus must absorb ready-made nutrients from elsewhere. A lichen is an association to their mutual (symbiotic) advantage between an alga and a fungus.

Under the protective surface layer of closely interwoven fungal threads, a layer of algal cells is supported by an open fungal matrix, modified lower down for attachment. The fungus draws food from the alga; the alga is protected by the fungus. Both can live separately but only in shady, wet places. Yet the combination may flourish on rock slopes facing the midday sun. The fruiting bodies pitting the surface release only fungal spores. The reproduction of the partnership depends upon powdery granules containing a few algal cells bound together by fungal threads being detached and then catching in a little crack.

Along a rocky shore the splash zone is dominated by lichens. The intertidal black layer (so often mistaken for oil) merges upwards into an orange and then the grey zone which reaches into the flowering plants. Nitrogen dropped by seabirds stimulates colour and quantity.

Ramalina siliquosa

Lecanora atra

Ochrolechia parella

Caloplaca marina

Xanthoria parietina

Pseudophyscia fusca

Verrucaria maura

Lichina confinis

Rocky Shore:
Splash Zone – flowers

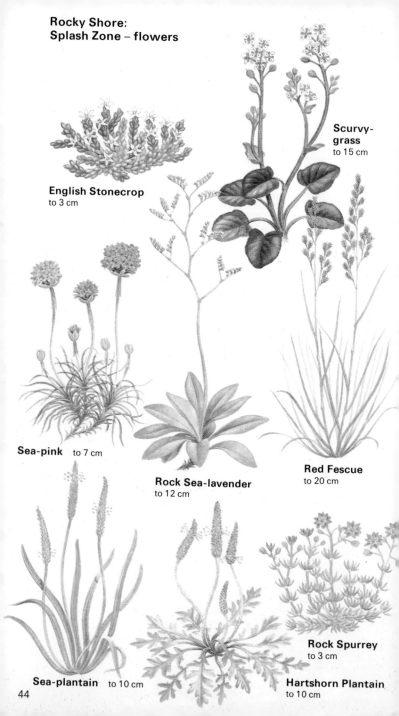

Scurvy-grass
to 15 cm

English Stonecrop
to 3 cm

Sea-pink   to 7 cm

Rock Sea-lavender
to 12 cm

Red Fescue
to 20 cm

Sea-plantain   to 10 cm

Hartshorn Plantain
to 10 cm

Rock Spurrey
to 3 cm

Sea-spleenwort
to 30 cm

Rock Samphire
to 30 cm

Golden Samphire
to 30–40 cm

The flowering plants that reach lowest into the splash zone are commonly exposed to salt spray and occasionally to green water. The water held in the rock will often be salt; yet the living material of these plants is not damaged. They are termed 'halophytes' (Gk. *halos*, sea salt). So few species can survive salt that lack of competition for space promotes survivors' abundance. Where most 'spray halophytes' also flourish inland where no salt reaches them, **Rock Samphire**, **Rock Spurrey** and **Rock Sea-lavender** cannot do so.

The problem of maintaining salt-balance in the tissues of estuarine animals is outlined on p.106. Suffice here to add that the root-hair cells of halophytes act as a membrane. When rain-waterlogged, surplus water is eliminated through the leaves; when salt-waterlogged, loss from the plant back into the salt is prevented by high internal salt, reduced transpiration and fleshy structural barriers.

Adaptations to resist hot drought include the deeply probing roots of **Sea-pink** or thrift, Rock Samphire and **Sea-spleenwort**. Hairs covering the plantains reflect heat and trap dew. **Stonecrops** have large cells specially for storing water. These plants are sustained by minimal humus trapped in cracks; gravity and rain bring down refuse and animal droppings, wind blows up detritus.

The **Sea-spleenwort**, the only maritime fern, lives in caves and crevices. The distribution of **Golden Samphire** and **Rock Sea-lavender** is strangely discontinuous. A little Rock Samphire adds an aromatic *je ne sais quoi* to a salad. Nearly all these plants recur in saltmarsh/shingle/dune communities.

Rocky Shore: Exposed

The angle of slope of very exposed shores profoundly modifies the populations that live on them. Surf washes across the gentler slopes daily and often violently; no large seaweed and few animals can survive. Particularly on some Atlantic coasts mussels may be overwhelmingly extensive: on other coasts barnacles dominate the scene (p.38). Nobody understands why, in a particular case, the one and not the other or a mixture of the two succeeds so prominently. Perhaps a refined analysis of mussel-shaped resistance to subtle variations in weight, frequency and angle of wave-wash may unravel the mystery.

Where mussels are few, barnacles abound. A maximum density of some 100,000 per sq. m. towards the top of the zone from which, going northwards, the warm water *Chthamalus* progressively disappears, making room for *Balanus balanoides* to go higher. Up to 200 small limpets per sq. m. may flourish amongst the barnacles. Tiny winkles amongst dead barnacles, an occasional dogwhelk and beadlet anemone are secured in clefts. Few other animals find shelter against the weight of wavewash.

Amongst the seaweeds only *Lithothamnion* (p.54) survives the full force of the waves. *Corallina* (p.54) and tufts of *Gigartina*, wrapped in the sea-mat *Flustrella*, succeed in minimal shelter.

Alaria is just above the oarweeds, increasingly common farther north and with the fruiting 'keys' conspicuous above the holdfast. The button stage of **Thongweed** grows through the winter. The thongs, which are the reproductive parts, develop in the first summer and release spores during the second. The few female 'oospheres' that fall where they are not immediately washed away chemically attract male 'spermatozoids' from the swimming swarm. The holdfast quickly follows fertilisation and a new button develops.

Thongweed
button to 6 cm
thong 30–150 cm

*Alaria
esculenta*
40–150 cm

Gigartina stellata
8–20 cm

Common mussel
3–8 cm

*Flustrella
hispida*

Rocky Shore: Exposed Gully

Apoglossum ruscifolium
8–15 cm

Purse Sponge
2–5 cm

Membranoptera alata
7–12 (–20) cm

Plumaria elegans
4–10 cm

48

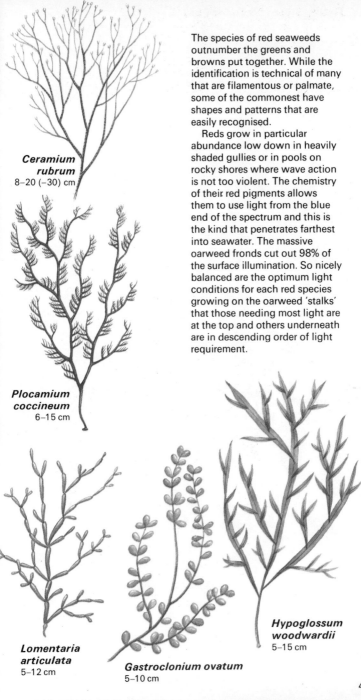

Ceramium rubrum
8–20 (–30) cm

The species of red seaweeds outnumber the greens and browns put together. While the identification is technical of many that are filamentous or palmate, some of the commonest have shapes and patterns that are easily recognised.

Reds grow in particular abundance low down in heavily shaded gullies or in pools on rocky shores where wave action is not too violent. The chemistry of their red pigments allows them to use light from the blue end of the spectrum and this is the kind that penetrates farthest into seawater. The massive oarweed fronds cut out 98% of the surface illumination. So nicely balanced are the optimum light conditions for each red species growing on the oarweed 'stalks' that those needing most light are at the top and others underneath are in descending order of light requirement.

Plocamium coccineum
6–15 cm

Hypoglossum woodwardii
5–15 cm

Lomentaria articulata
5–12 cm

Gastroclonium ovatum
5–10 cm

49

Rocky Shore: Exposed Pool

Phycodrys rubens
to 20 cm

Delesseria sanguinea
to 20 cm

Heterosiphonia plumosa
15–30 cm

Calliblepharis sp.
10–15 cm

Common Prawn
4–8 cm

Callophyllis laciniata
5–10 cm

Aesop Prawn
2–6 cm

50

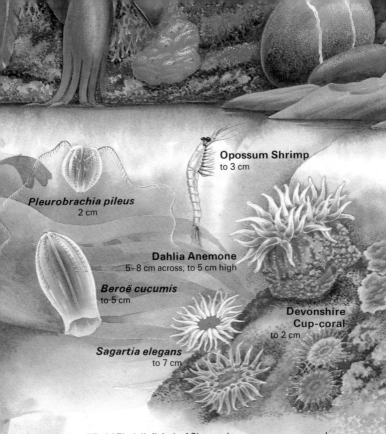

Opossum Shrimp to 3 cm

Pleurobrachia pileus 2 cm

Dahlia Anemone 5–8 cm across; to 5 cm high

Beroë cucumis to 5 cm

Devonshire Cup-coral to 2 cm

Sagartia elegans to 7 cm

Hydroids (pp.55, 117), jellyfish (p.18), corals, sea-anemones and sea-gooseberries all belong to the same division of the animal kingdom, the Coelenterata (Gk. *coel*, hollow; *enteron*, gut). Their simple bodies have only two layers of cells but include a nerve network. Extremely common, most are circular. They all have a simple pouch in which digestion occurs and to which the single entrance acts as both mouth and anus. All are carnivorous. Except in the sea-gooseberries, the tentacles, usually round the mouth, have stinging cells which paralyse their prey and so prevent damage to their own bodies at the time of 'swallowing'.

Many anemones are hermaphrodite. Most release eggs and sperm for fertilisation in the sea. In others fertilisation is internal and miniature near-adults emerge. Hydroids are effectively colonies of tiny anemones attached in patterns to a communal jointed 'stalk'. Tentacles from each translucent cup rhythmically beat a stream of water into the cup to supply food and oxygen. The sea-gooseberries swim by beating their eight meridian rows of irridescent plates. *Pleurobrachia* lassoes its food while itself being engulfed by the much larger *Beroë* as it progresses, open mouth forwards.

Rocky Shore: Sheltered Gully

The **Dogwhelk** is adapted to survive through a wide range of exposure. On sheltered shores the shell is finely spired and intricately ridged, the lip is thin and mouth small. In increasing exposure the shell becomes thicker, blunter and smoother and the mouth occupies a greater proportion of the smaller length. Individuals taken from the two ends of this gradation ('cline') would not be recognised as belonging to the same species.

Dogwhelks eat barnacles. Their hollow tubular tongue, extruded down the rolled prolongation of the shell, is armed with teeth which bore through the barnacles' central plates, exposing the meat to be sucked up through the tube. Three or four little lumps in the adult's mouth develop when near-starvation prevents steady growth. When food is plentiful again, shell growth restarts, carrying the lumps up into the body-whorl.

The risks inherent in planktonic development are avoided by adults congregating in cracks to copulate. The females then deposit egg capsules, each containing 300 to 1,000 eggs of which only 2–3% are fertile. After four months some dozen dogwhelks emerge, 1–2 mm long, having eaten the 97% infertile eggs.

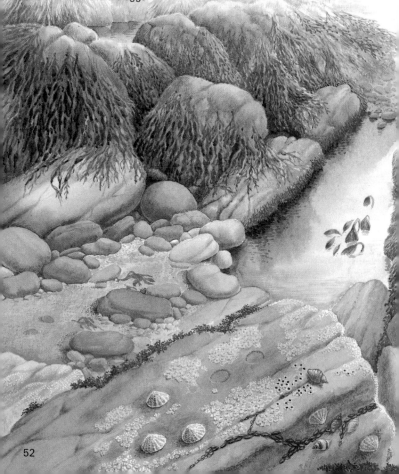

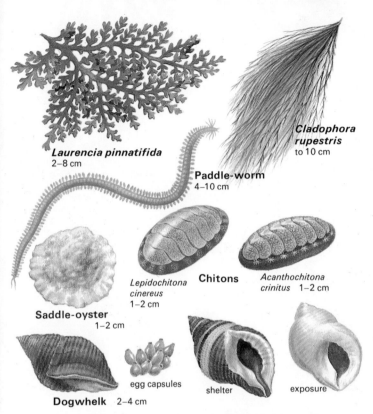

Laurencia pinnatifida
2–8 cm

Paddle-worm
4–10 cm

Cladophora rupestris
to 10 cm

Chitons

Lepidochitona cinereus
1–2 cm

Acanthochitona crinitus 1–2 cm

Saddle-oyster
1–2 cm

Dogwhelk 2–4 cm

egg capsules

shelter

exposure

Large wracks dominate sheltered shores: the physical violence of wave action excludes them from exposed coasts. One extreme grades into the other through a series of mosaic shores with larger to smaller patches of seaweed between smaller to larger areas dominated by barnacles. Limpets are the intermediate control of the pattern.

Limpets feed when the tide is in. They slide along, rasping off the rocks the fine seaweed film developing from spores just settled after fertilisation in the plankton. Limpets also have larval stages. At their final metamorphosis to adults those which sink onto rocks within reach of the waving wracks are brushed off. As shelter increases so does the radius of wrack-sweep, causing limpets and barnacles to decrease.

By twisting this way and that, a limpet grinds its shell to fit hard rock or grinds soft rock to fit its shell so exactly that water trapped within cannot seep out over low tide. However the shell can be raised just enough to admit air from which oxygen diffuses through the shell-water to the gills. From each foray each limpet must – and does – return to its own 'home'. The power to clamp down tight gives security against predators (gulls, oystercatchers) and, more important, against waves.

Purple encrustations. In rock pools and low on exposed rocky shores nothing is more conspicuous than the widespread pink-mauve encrustations built by the family of red seaweeds which can separate from seawater lime and magnesium, the whiteness of which modifies the purple-red plant pigments. The process of separation remains a mystery.

The Lithophyllum–Lithothamnion group forms these stone-hard crusts on the rocks (Gk. *lithos*, a stone; *phullon*, a leaf; *thamnos*, a branch). The differences between the 21 British species are largely in the shape and number of pores through which the spores emerge. Their colour bleaches fast when exposed to direct sunlight: hence the white rim round higher level pools.

The Corallina group of many-branched plants has only the narrow joints uncalcified, so giving some flexibility to combat wavewash. White specks at the tips indicate the internal 'skeleton'.

Until the mid-19th century these plants were classified as corals. Particularly in the Pacific, they are preserved through hundreds of metres deep as fossils; veritable rock-builders. Indeed, many coral reefs and islands are massed fossilised seaweeds almost without true corals. Some are still getting larger, still without corals.

Sea Lettuce
10–20 cm

Wartlet or **Gem anemone**
1–4 cm

strawberry variety

Coralweed
5–10 cm

Lithophyllum spp.

Beadlet
3 cm

Snakelocks
to 3 cm

Springtail
3 mm

Rocky Shore: Hazards of Midtide Pools

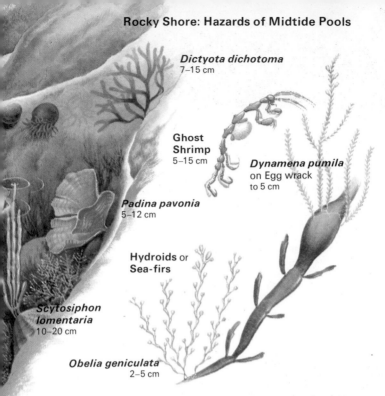

Dictyota dichotoma
7–15 cm

Ghost Shrimp
5–15 cm

Dynamena pumila
on Egg wrack
to 5 cm

Padina pavonia
5–12 cm

Hydroids or **Sea-firs**

Scytosiphon lomentaria
10–20 cm

Obelia geniculata
2–5 cm

Rock pools do not shelter the lovely variety of life they are generally imagined to, nor are they necessarily a safe refuge for sea creatures stranded by the ebb tide. Many shore animals are excluded from them because they cannot survive continuous submersion in seawater. However, large, deep, shaded pools allow some marine organisms to live above low water. Higher up, and particularly in smaller pools, the water temperature varies widely with the season and the angle and hours of exposure to the sun. Salinity increases with evaporation and decreases in heavy rain. The arrival of the flood tide produces physiological shock as both factors abruptly return to 'normal'. Increasing temperature raises the rates of photosynthesis (p.14) and respiration. So the oxygen and carbon dioxide dissolved in the water and its pH (acidity) also vary with the pool's temperature and illumination. On gentler slopes, pebbles stirred by waves grind all life from the rock surface. Perhaps the wonder is that pools contain as much as they do.

The wingless insect *Anurida maritima* shelters in cracks, scavenging dead titbits, and is common on the surface of little pools. All insects breathe atmospheric oxygen. The cross section of the tiny holes through which *Anurida* inhales is so small that the surface tension of seawater prevents penetration into the insect's body or it would be drowned. If carried down by wave backwash into a cold water layer, they survive for up to five days breathing air trapped in the fine hairs which cover their bodies. So, in a manner, one breath every five days ensures survival.

Rocky Shore: Sheltered Pool. Seaweeds

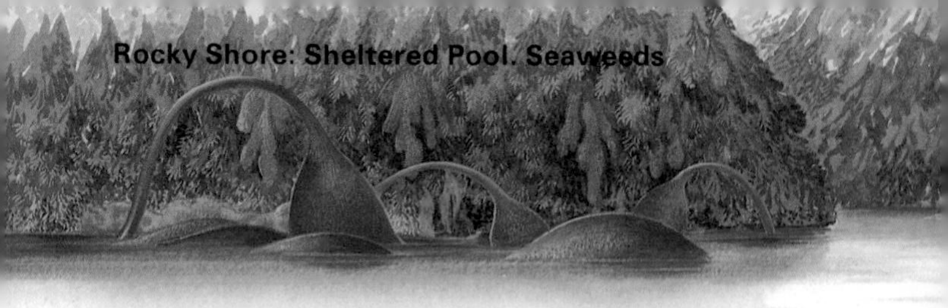

Seaweeds are nowhere more abundant than in these larger steep-sided lower shore pools, particularly those in the warm water southwest, where ***Bifurcaria*** lies along the surface, deepening the shade.

Where conifers and flowering plants bear multicellular seeds within which are complicated plant embryos, the 'lower' plants (fungi, mosses, ferns and algae) produce single-celled spores whose development follows their release from the parent.

Three groups of seaweeds (algae) are obvious on the shore – the Greens, Browns and Reds. They all possess chlorophyll which enables them to use the energy of the sun (photosynthesis p.14). Reds live lowest as they use light at the blue end of the spectrum which penetrates deepest into the sea. The Greens live higher on the shore, using red light which does not penetrate far into seawater. The Browns use light from a wider band of wavelengths.

Alas, nothing is simple. The colour of some healthy plants is red-brown and others brown-green. Unhealthy Reds turn green: dead Reds and Greens are white.

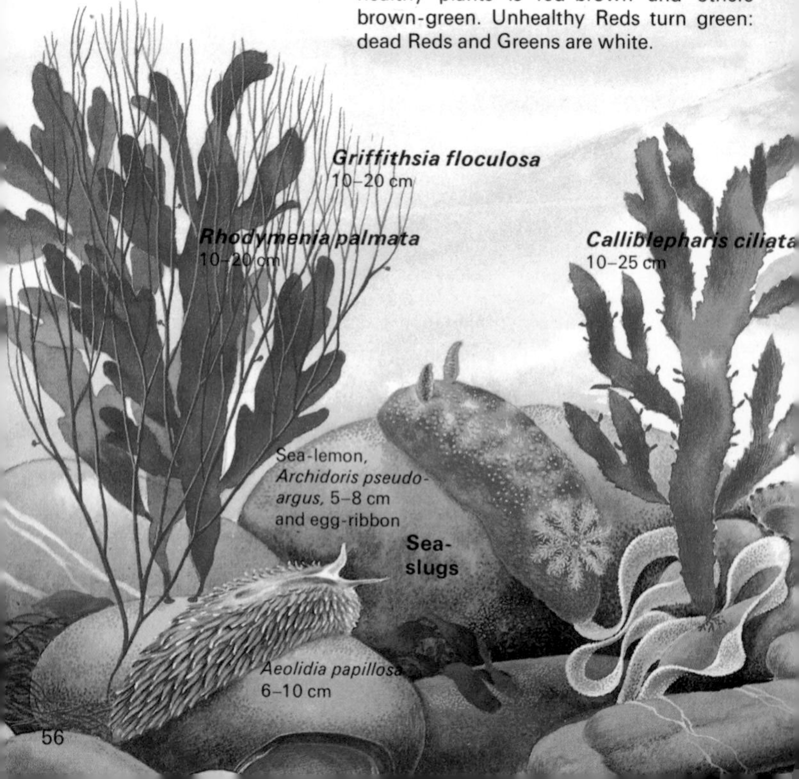

Griffithsia floculosa
10–20 cm
Rhodymenia palmata
10–20 cm
Calliblepharis ciliata
10–25 cm
Sea-lemon,
Archidoris pseudo-argus, 5–8 cm
and egg-ribbon
Sea-slugs
Aeolidia papillosa
6–10 cm

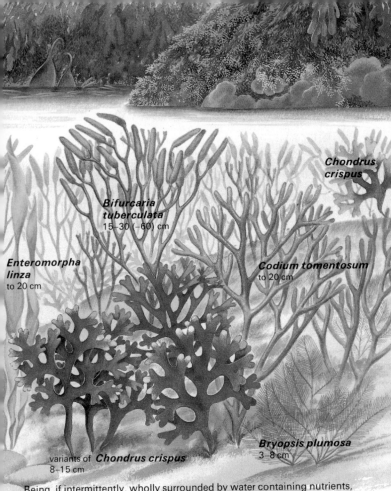

Chondrus crispus

Bifurcaria tuberculata
15–30 (–60) cm

Enteromorpha linza
to 20 cm

Codium tomentosum
to 20 cm

variants of *Chondrus crispus*
8–15 cm

Bryopsis plumosa
3–8 cm

Being, if intermittently, wholly surrounded by water containing nutrients, seaweeds do not need an elaborate root system to gather and transmit food throughout the plant. The higher up the shore, the thicker the cell walls, giving greater capacity for retaining moisture. However, seaweeds need attachment firm enough to combat waves.

Some 'holdfasts' are root-like, either a few 'rhizoids' or more complex interlocking structures; some grow as tufts; and yet others are disc-shaped, either hard, as in the wracks, or more loosely interwoven plates.

The frond ('thallus') of the mature plants may be crustaceous, like *Lithothamnion* (p.54); cylindrical, either thread-fine single filaments or thicker, flexible rods of many threads growing together; or flattened, palmate, membraneous or leaf-like. Some are undivided, some variously lobed or branched in regular patterns, but none has a cellular complexity comparable to that of flowering plants.

Rocky Shore: Sheltered – Sponges, Sea-squirts and Worms

About 250 sponge species grow in British waters, few of them above mean sea level. Nowhere are they more prominent than at the bottom of rocky shores, particularly under and low on the sides of overhangs and boulders too big to be moved by the waves.

Simple, primitive animals, they draw in through many minute pores a stream of water from which they take oxygen and plankton-food. Carbon dioxide and body wastes are expelled through fewer larger holes which, in some species, are shared by a group of individuals fused in the one mass. The 'body' of the mass is stiffened by hard splinter-like needles of silica or lime. All sponges reproduce sexually. Sperm enters with the inflow water; fertilised eggs change into larvae which are expelled into the plankton with the outflow where they develop until the time for change to adult attachment.

The **Star Ascidian** is not a sponge but a colonial sea-squirt (tunicate, p.116). Each segment is a separate animal with its own inlet; the central outlet is shared by all the animals in the star. Sexual conjunction produces 'tadpole' larvae with a stiff flexible rod strengthening their length and a single nerve chord, enlarged at the head end (i.e. vestigial backbone, central nervous system and brain). This evidence of evolution disappears when the 'tail' is shed as the tadpole fixes itself on its head to become an adult.

Breadcrumb-sponge

Star Ascidian

Hymeniacidon sanguinea

Myxilla incrustans

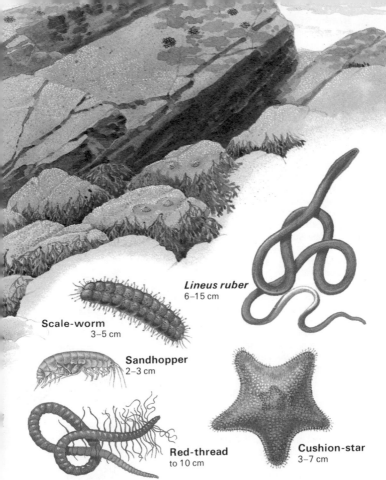

Lineus ruber
6–15 cm

Scale-worm
3–5 cm

Sandhopper
2–3 cm

Red-thread
to 10 cm

Cushion-star
3–7 cm

Overlapping plates covered in bristles protect the respiratory openings of scavenging scale-worms. Under stones firmly bedded on smelly mud/sand, the common **Red-thread** lies buried except for the red filaments protruding into the surface water to aerate the blood, while longer filaments carry back algal spores, diatoms and organic debris from which the edible is selected by mouth-flaps. These worms emerge in large numbers to breed in unison, depositing yellowish jelly-eggs.

The unsegmented carnivorous **Lineus** lives in the same habitat. Tiny bristle-worms are lassoed by an evertible proboscis and ingested whole. These Nemerteans are the lowest group to have evolved a digestive tract with both mouth and anus and a blood circulation made efficient by haemoglobin. The sexes are separate. Eggs hatch within the females before ejection as planktonic larvae.

Sandhoppers abound here too.

Rocky Shore: Crabs

Crabs live from MSL downwards along rocky coasts wherever boulders, overhangs and seaweeds provide shelter. When a leg is trapped under a stone rolled onto it by waves during a gale, the crab avoids starvation by casting off that leg by muscular contraction and quickly grows a replacement within the stump.

Having a skeleton outside the body, growth requires periodical moulting ('ecdysis'). The crab crawls into deep shelter and swallows so much water that internal pressure splits the shell around the back which then hinges open. In 2–3 hours the soft crab pulls out backwards, legs to their tip-ends, feelers and eyes from their stalks, gills from their covers. Then, in 3–4 days, a new shell hardens, a third larger than its predecessor. Regenerated legs open from the stump of the old. Although waves pulverise most cast shells, many accumulate in quiet corners along the tideline.

The granular mass of roughly 150,000 eggs is carried under the female's tail for several months before hatching into planktonic larvae, then passing through six changes of form before emerging as a 'crab', about 3 mm across.

A fleshy yellow bag under the tail of a Shore Crab is the body of a parasitic barnacle, *Sacculina* from which threads penetrate throughout the host, to the tips of its legs and eye-stalks, which absorb the body fluids of the host and inhibit ecdysis. *Sacculina* dies after releasing its own eggs when full vitality returns to the Shore Crab.

Most crabs feed on lumps torn off their prey with their nippers; but **Porcelain Crabs** rhythmically evert and suck in again a mouth-bag covered in fine hairs which trap plankton. The fifth pair of Porcelains' legs is minute and tucked tightly across the base of its tail. The Broad-clawed's body hairs are wriggled into muddy sand to give firm anchorage.

The last two joints on the **Swimming Crab's** back legs are flattened as a paddle. Nobody knows why some small **Shore Crabs** have symmetrical white patterns on their shells.

Broad-clawed Porcelain Crab
to 2 cm

Long-clawed Porcelain Crab
5 mm

Xantho incisus
to 5 cm

Hairy Crab
to 3 cm

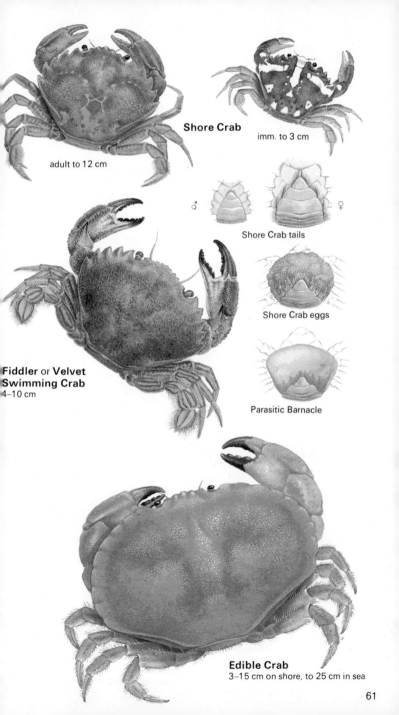

Shore Crab

imm. to 3 cm

adult to 12 cm

♂ ♀

Shore Crab tails

Shore Crab eggs

Parasitic Barnacle

Fiddler or **Velvet Swimming Crab**
4–10 cm

Edible Crab
3–15 cm on shore, to 25 cm in sea

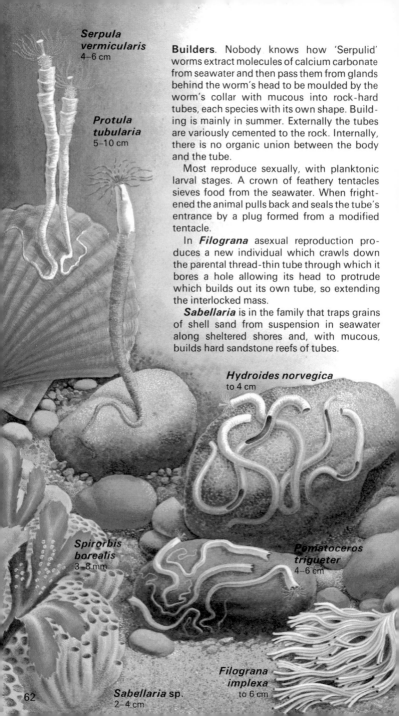

**Serpula
vermicularis**
4–6 cm

**Protula
tubularia**
5–10 cm

Builders. Nobody knows how 'Serpulid'
worms extract molecules of calcium carbonate
from seawater and then pass them from glands
behind the worm's head to be moulded by the
worm's collar with mucous into rock-hard
tubes, each species with its own shape. Building is mainly in summer. Externally the tubes
are variously cemented to the rock. Internally,
there is no organic union between the body
and the tube.

Most reproduce sexually, with planktonic
larval stages. A crown of feathery tentacles
sieves food from the seawater. When fright-
ened the animal pulls back and seals the tube's
entrance by a plug formed from a modified
tentacle.

In **Filograna** asexual reproduction produces a new individual which crawls down
the parental thread-thin tube through which it
bores a hole allowing its head to protrude
which builds out its own tube, so extending
the interlocked mass.

Sabellaria is in the family that traps grains
of shell sand from suspension in seawater
along sheltered shores and, with mucous,
builds hard sandstone reefs of tubes.

Hydroides norvegica
to 4 cm

**Spirorbis
borealis**
3–8 mm

**Pomatoceros
trigueter**
4–6 cm

**Filograna
implexa**
to 6 cm

62

Sabellaria sp.
2–4 cm

Rocky Shore: Borers and Builders

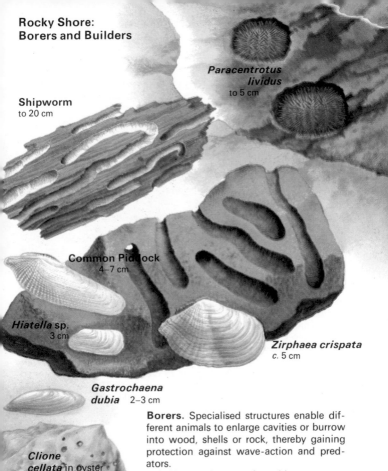

Paracentrotus lividus
to 5 cm

Shipworm
to 20 cm

Common Piddock
4–7 cm

Hiatella sp.
3 cm

Zirphaea crispata
c. 5 cm

Gastrochaena dubia 2–3 cm

Clione cellata in oyster

Polydora sp.
to 10 mm

Borers. Specialised structures enable different animals to enlarge cavities or burrow into wood, shells or rock, thereby gaining protection against wave-action and predators.

Acid secretion cuts branching passages into shells for the sponge *Cliona* and U-shaped tubes, with their mud extensions, for the worm *Polydora*.

By slowly twisting hard spines and teeth the sea-urchin *Paracentrotus* enlarges a hollow. Anchored by muscular adherence of their foot, piddocks rasp rock or wood by twisting spines on their shells. *Hiatella* excavates by twisting its shell forced open by internal water pressure.

The shipworm (which is a mollusc), anchored by its sucker-foot, rocks unhinged valves armed with efficient 'teeth' to excavate its burrow, later given a hard calcareous lining.

Rocky Shore: Oarweed Forest, low tide

Of all the plants and animals in the oarweed forest none are commoner than **Sea-mats** living on the fronds. Each cell in each honeycomb houses a single animal which extends an arc of delicate tentacles when feeding underwater. The labels Polyzoa (= many animals) and Bryozoa (= moss animals) are synonyms. Each individual has a U-shaped gut, the mouth within the arc of tentacles and the anus outside it. The tentacles are covered with vibratile hairs, beating to draw in a current of water for oxygen and food (suspension feeding; pp.75, 80).

Nearly all Polyzoa are hermaphrodite, with male and female gonads in the same cell. The process of fertilisation is a mystery. After a short time in the plankton, larvae settle and undergo their last metamorphosis into a 'cell', appropriately called the 'ancestrulum', from which others bud off in a way nobody understands. The cell wall may be stiffened with lime. Two colonies never fuse when they come together, even though their ancestrula may have come from the same parent: but two arms of the same colony readily do fuse.

An animal dead in its cell degenerates into a little hard 'brown body'. A replacement emerges from the cell wall, its gut enveloping the brown body which then passes out of the new anus. So the vitality of the individual colony persists until the host plant dies: but the continuity of the species is secured by settlement of larvae produced sexually.

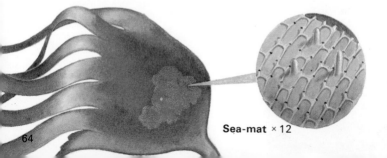

Sea-mat × 12

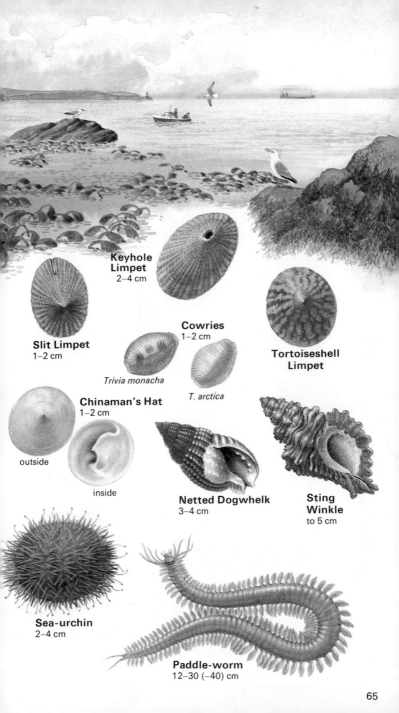

Keyhole Limpet
2–4 cm

Slit Limpet
1–2 cm

Cowries
1–2 cm

Trivia monacha

T. arctica

Tortoiseshell Limpet

Chinaman's Hat
1–2 cm

outside

inside

Netted Dogwhelk
3–4 cm

Sting Winkle
to 5 cm

Sea-urchin
2–4 cm

Paddle-worm
12–30 (–40) cm

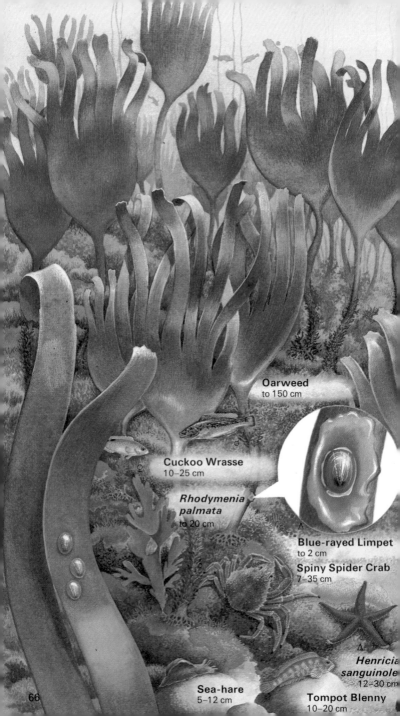

Oarweed
to 150 cm

Cuckoo Wrasse
10–25 cm

*Rhodymenia
palmata*
to 20 cm

Blue-rayed Limpet
to 2 cm

Spiny Spider Crab
7–35 cm

*Henricia
sanguinole*
12–30 cm

Sea-hare
5–12 cm

Tompot Blenny
10–20 cm

Rocky Shore: Oarweed Forest, high tide

Blue-rayed Limpets are closely related to Commons (p.52). Fertilisation depends on sperm meeting egg in the sea. Larvae hatch in winter and change into 5 mm adults in May.

Many lodge on **Oarweed** fronds, to feed on their surface layer and diatoms settled on it. The shell secures them against wave-action, its irridescent lines coloured by sunlight chemistry.

In autumn, the outer half of the oarweed, having performed its reproductive function, begins to rot. Warned by the changing taste of their food, the limpets migrate to safety low on the frond. Next spring they travel up again as the frond develops new reproductive parts. Few survive longer than one year.

Those which chance originally carried inside the holdfasts develop a thick, tough, tall shell. A third group move from their first frond-settlement to inside the holdfast, the stage of moving showing clearly where the original thin, clean shell thickens and roughens.

The lump of residual shell in the middle of a **Sea-hare**'s back characterises that group of sea-slugs less evolved than the shell-less ones on p.56 and p.113. A defensive cloud of purple ink is emitted when disturbed.

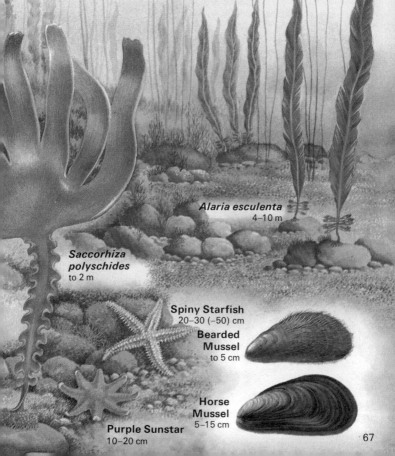

Alaria esculenta
4–10 m

Saccorhiza polyschides
to 2 m

Spiny Starfish
20–30 (–50) cm

Bearded Mussel
to 5 cm

Horse Mussel
5–15 cm

Purple Sunstar
10–20 cm

Rocky Shore: Oarweed Forest, high tide

Starfish are exclusively marine, with essentially radial symmetry and an articulated 'skeleton' of calcareous plates which enlarge as the animal grows. The sexes are separate. Synchronised spawning leads to fertilisation in seawater. Several planktonic stages precede adult settlement.

Near the centre of the upper side is a large pore covered by a sieve-plate through which cilia draw seawater into circulation. This penetrates down lines extending along the arms, to which are connected a myriad of 'tube-feet' projecting on either side of grooves. Muscular pressure distends these feet, giving progressive adherence to their terminal suckers. Having no front or back, whichever arm points in the preferred direction then takes the lead.

Starfish eat mussels and scallops. Suction from relays of tube-feet force the mollusc valves slowly apart. The predator then enwraps the mollusc in its large stomach which is protruded inside out through its tiny mouth and so digests the mollusc outside the starfish body.

If damaged during a storm, new arms are quickly regenerated. A single arm attached to but half a disc will be restored to a whole animal.

Shore Crab
4–10 cm

*Galathea
squamifera*
3–6 cm

Squat Lobsters

*Galathea
strigosa*
6–10 cm

Underside of
Palmipes membranaceus
8–15 cm

Porania pulvillus
5–10 cm

True lobsters and warmer water crawfish have powerful, rounded bodies. The first of five pairs of walking legs may carry strong pinchers. Squat-lobsters have oval, flattened bodies, with the fifth pair of legs folded within the gill chamber under the tail.

Lobsters weigh up to 15 kg, of which half may be claw. Active at night, but too slow to capture live food, they mostly scavenge (hence dead meat as bait in pots); some are cannibals. Crawfish eat small snails, warding off intruders with their hard flexible antennae covered in needle-sharp spines.

Lobsters spawn every second year. Males deposit sperm in pockets on the underside of females whose eggs are then fertilised and laid in July and August. After ten months' incubation beneath the female abdomen the 'berry' hatches, to spend 6–8 weeks as planktonic larvae before sheltering under stones as minute adults. These moult 14–17 times during their first year and 25 times to attain a length of 25 cm after five years.

Squat-lobsters digest larger organic debris from suspension in water, sucked in through their mouths. How indigestible solids are rejected is a mystery.

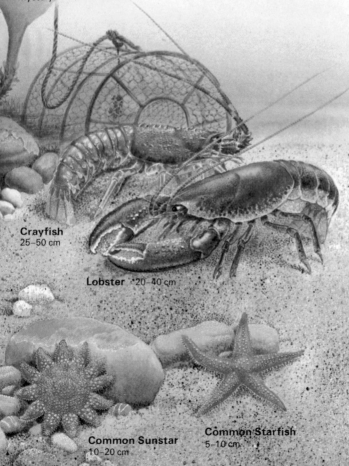

Crayfish
25–50 cm

Lobster 20–40 cm

Common Sunstar
10–20 cm

Common Starfish
5–10 cm

Three-bearded Rockling
8–30 cm

Common Blenny or Shanny
8–12 cm

Butterfly Blenny
8–12 cm

Desmarestia ligulata
50–150 cm

Montagu's Sea-snail
5–10 cm

Cornish Sucker
5–10 cm

Two-spotted Sucker
3–5 cm

More than twenty species of fish live amongst seaweeds and jumbled stones low down on rocky shores. All are teleosts (p.9), although some have no scales.

Blennies have teeth and neck muscles powerful enough to scrape barnacles off the rocks for food. Indeed they can hold themselves horizontal from a bite onto a finger. Sandhoppers, little molluscs and crabs are chewed up too.

Their relatives the **Butterfish** eat small crustacea and worms. In winter they lay clumps of yellow eggs in a shell or under a stone, guarded by an adult until they hatch in March. Young grow to 8 cm in their second and to 14 cm in their fourth year.

Fatherlashers (Sea-scorpions) are poor swimmers but so effectively camouflaged that small crustacea and fish can be enveloped in a lunging gulp after a stealthy stalk. Sudden raising of the spiny gill cover startles off predators who penetrate the camouflage.

By having the two pelvic fins fused to form a sucking disc for attachment to rocks, all the dozen or more species of goby survive heavier exposure than most shore fish. Additional security comes from lying deep amongst the mass of small seaweeds, camouflaged so accurately that many think gobies are scarce. Where most species are gregarious, the **Rock Goby** is rather solitary, yet common.

The cold water **Sea-snail** and the warm water, flattened **Suckers** also have pelvic pads. Little sandhoppers are the favoured food of Sea-snails but what Suckers eat is unknown. The Snails lay eggs amongst hydroids (p.51) in May/June and the Suckers guard theirs, golden and fixed in empty shells, in July/August. All have planktonic larvae. Suckers move down to 30 m deep in cold winters.

Rock Goby
10 cm

Fatherlasher
10–25 cm

Butterfish
7–10 (–20) cm

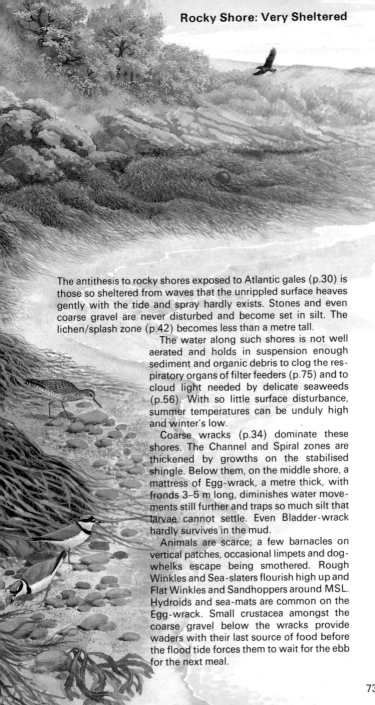

The antithesis to rocky shores exposed to Atlantic gales (p.30) is those so sheltered from waves that the unrippled surface heaves gently with the tide and spray hardly exists. Stones and even coarse gravel are never disturbed and become set in silt. The lichen/splash zone (p.42) becomes less than a metre tall.

The water along such shores is not well aerated and holds in suspension enough sediment and organic debris to clog the respiratory organs of filter feeders (p.75) and to cloud light needed by delicate seaweeds (p.56). With so little surface disturbance, summer temperatures can be unduly high and winter's low.

Coarse wracks (p.34) dominate these shores. The Channel and Spiral zones are thickened by growths on the stabilised shingle. Below them, on the middle shore, a mattress of Egg-wrack, a metre thick, with fronds 3–5 m long, diminishes water movements still further and traps so much silt that larvae cannot settle. Even Bladder-wrack hardly survives in the mud.

Animals are scarce; a few barnacles on vertical patches, occasional limpets and dog-whelks escape being smothered. Rough Winkles and Sea-slaters flourish high up and Flat Winkles and Sandhoppers around MSL. Hydroids and sea-mats are common on the Egg-wrack. Small crustacea amongst the coarse gravel below the wracks provide waders with their last source of food before the flood tide forces them to wait for the ebb for the next meal.

Sandy/Muddy Shore

Empty space in a boxful of balls is 25% of the volume of the box. Where coarser sand is mixed with finer particles of silt up to 45% of the volume would be 'interstitial space'. Capillary action draws water up through the interstitial spaces so that the water-table in sandy shores is well above tide level. The finer the particles, the higher the water rises. In the layers just above the water, the air in the spaces is water-saturated. Exactly the same principle supplies water to sand-dune plants (p.88).

The forward rush of waves builds up the larger stones and coarser sand round the top of a bay. The backwash drags down only the finer (p.89). The degree to which a sandy shore is exposed to wave action determines the angle of slope and the size of particles on it. On exposed sandy beaches the particles of sand are so much ground together by the waves that life cannot survive amongst them. Minimal shelter from gales allows smaller grains of sand, fragments of shell and even traces of silt and organic refuse to mix with the coarser silica grains. Some diatoms (p.15) and microscopic animals now do survive in the spaces between grains and Banded Wedge-shell (p.78) the first large colonist.

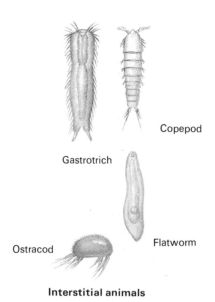

Copepod

Gastrotrich

Ostracod

Flatworm

Interstitial animals

In bays further sheltered from all large waves, the particles of silt, clay and decaying organic matter derived from dead seaweeds and animals and leaves from overhanging trees increasingly dominate the sand. The angle of slope becomes ever gentler until the sequence ends in mud flats.

Bacteria feeding on the organic refuse use up the oxygen and produce smelly hydrogen sulphide. Fine mud is sloppy because the tiny capillaries bring so much water to the surface. Though these fine particles clog unadapted respiratory mechanisms, the organic refuse is food for large populations as different from those living in firm sand as the sand is from the mud.

Burrowing downwards in these substrates is mechanically easy, but many animals, notably molluscs and worms, are advantaged beyond just security from predators. Great heat and hard frost penetrate only a few centimetres before the equable flood tide returns. Deeper than 10 cm, salinity of water in sand/mud hardly varies. Rain or a stream do not penetrate below the surface.

The bodies of bivalve molluscs (i.e. those with two parts to their shells – cockles and mussels) have two extensible tubes (siphons) which can be pushed up to the surface. These siphons may be united in one column or separate. The 'suspension feeders' are those which draw down more or less clean water through the inhalant siphon. The 'deposit feeders' use the inhalant siphon as a surface suction-dredger.

Suspension and deposit feeders

In both cases the inedible is sieved off, the edible ingested and the contained oxygen respired. Digestive wastes and the sieved-off detritus are passed into the exhalant siphon, to be pumped out with sufficient force to clear the inhalant, so avoiding the danger of recycling used water.

In all molluscs the outside of a fold of tissue, the mantle, enclosing the organs of digestion, excretion, breathing and reproduction, is an integral part of the shell. Glands in the mantle secrete the shell material. Small layers of animal tissue are progressively sandwiched between thicker layers of minerals, mostly calcium carbonate, separated by the mollusc from seawater and its food. The minerals impregnate the animal tissue: the animal gives life to the mineral. If all the minerals were dissolved, the animal would be a thin, membraneous net.

When food is scarce, the energy ingested maintains life. A seasonal increase of food diverts surplus energy to renewed shell building, marked by prominent concentric 'growth' lines. Then, energy used to enlarge the animal to fit the bigger shell slows down the rate of shell growth. A crack across a shell may be repaired within twelve hours by adding new shelly matter.

The two 'valves' of bivalve shells are joined at the top, just 'behind' the beak or umbo, by a leathery, elastic, 'ligament'. Beneath the umbo is the hinge, with teeth to prevent one valve sliding across the other. When feeding the ligament presses the two valves open. When disturbed the shell is tightly shut by muscles whose impressions, together with a line along the limit of the 'mantle attachment', are clear marks in empty shells.

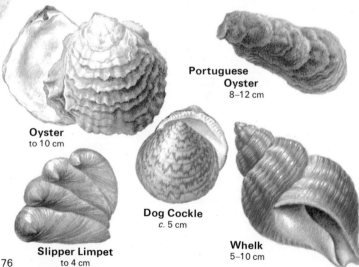

Portuguese Oyster
8–12 cm

Oyster
to 10 cm

Dog Cockle
c. 5 cm

Slipper Limpet
to 4 cm

Whelk
5–10 cm

Great Scallop
6–12 cm

Variegated Scallop
c. 4 cm

Carpet-shells

Venerupis rhomboides
4–6 cm

Venerupis pullastra
5 cm

Dosinia lupinus
3 cm

**Rayed Trough
Shell** to 5 cm

**Thick Trough
Shell**
4 cm

By day the **Masked Crab** is buried in sand, safe from predatory fish, with only tips of the antennae above the surface. Water (oxygen) is drawn down a tube formed by two rows of interlocking hairs on each antennae. The solids in this water would clog its respiratory mechanism did the crab not reverse the circulation when out of its burrow feeding at night.

The voracious **Burrowing Starfish** eats whole molluscs, worms, etc. It sinks vertically down into sand through which vibrating spines maintain open a respiratory tube to the surface. **Sand-eels** are buried just under the low-tide sand, sometimes in huge numbers. They eat plankton and tiny fish and are eaten by mackerel, cod, etc., and seabirds.

The **Lesser Weeverfish** sinks only half into the sand. It eats prawns and little fish, mostly at night. If stepped on, the poison from glands in the dorsal fin and gill covers produces intense pain, eased by bathing with hot water. Medical attention is often needed.

The carnivorous **Necklace Shell** is the only sand-burrowing snail, dissolving neat holes in bivalves with sulphuric acid secreted from its proboscis through which it then sucks the meat of its victim. The 'necklace' of eggs, cemented in sand grains by mucous, is commonly washed ashore.

Actaeon is a burrowing sea-slug in a group which has not yet lost its shell. **Gapers** live to 30 cm down in muddy sand from the Arctic to France, Japan and Carolina (clam chowder). **Sunset-shells**, in coarser sand/gravel, and **Venus**, in finer, occur from the Arctic Circle to Senegal

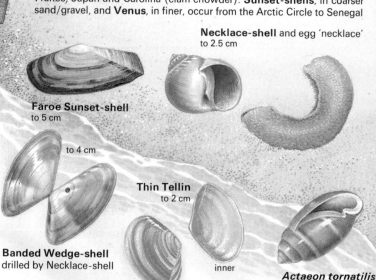

Necklace-shell and egg 'necklace'
to 2.5 cm

Faroe Sunset-shell
to 5 cm

to 4 cm

Thin Tellin
to 2 cm

Banded Wedge-shell
drilled by Necklace-shell

inner

outer

Actaeon tornatilis
to 2 cm

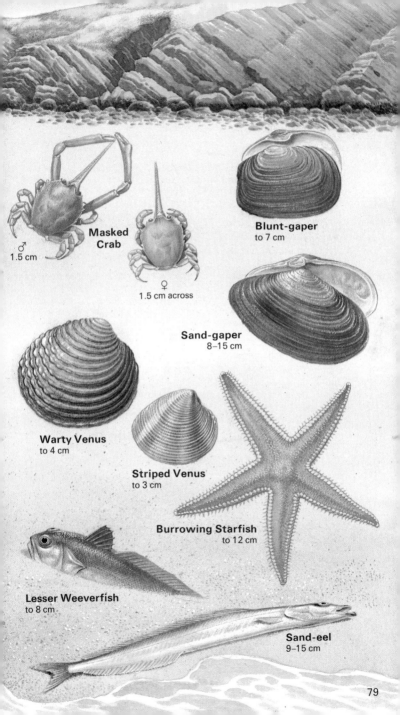

Masked Crab
♂
1.5 cm

♀
1.5 cm across

Blunt-gaper
to 7 cm

Sand-gaper
8–15 cm

Warty Venus
to 4 cm

Striped Venus
to 3 cm

Burrowing Starfish
to 12 cm

Lesser Weeverfish
to 8 cm

Sand-eel
9–15 cm

79

Sandy/Muddy Shore

Razorshells live vertically in cleanish sand with their two siphons at the surface. Pressure waves through the sand from approaching feet warn them to thrust down their own foot, expand it by blood pressure to a mushroom-anchor shape against which the animal can pull itself down and repeat the cycle so fast that it disappears too quickly to catch by digging. The initial muscular contraction spurts water from the body some 15 cm into the air. The reverse sequence drives the animal up again.

Pharus, a tellin, not a razorshell, exemplifies the development of an advantageous shape in two distinct types of animal – 'convergent evolution'. **Cockles** spend a brief larval period in the plankton before settling, as adults, up to 10,000 per sq. m., on sandy mud into which their powerful foot burrows some 4 cm, leaving their siphons at the surface for suspension feeding (p.75). In summer, when food is abundant, the shell grows larger. During winter, growth almost ceases and the next concentric 'age' ring develops. Anchorage comes from furrows and hooks on these thick shells.

The five grooves on the shell ('test') of the **Sea-potato** reveal its relationship to starfish. They live 10 cm down in sand. The burrowing sea-anemone *Peachia* is anchored at lowest tide by the bulbous bottom of its column. *Cereus*, variable in shape and colour, is attached to a shell or stone in muddy sand. The long arms of the **Brittle-star** anchor it some 10 cm down in sand. The **Ottershell** lives much deeper, its massive siphons joined in a thick, horny sheath.

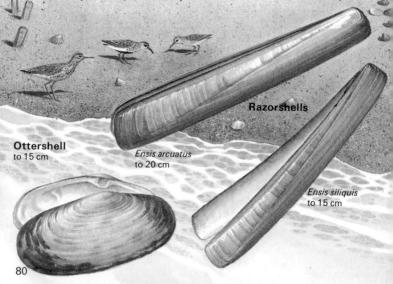

Razorshells

Ottershell
to 15 cm

Ensis arcuatus
to 20 cm

Ensis siliquis
to 15 cm

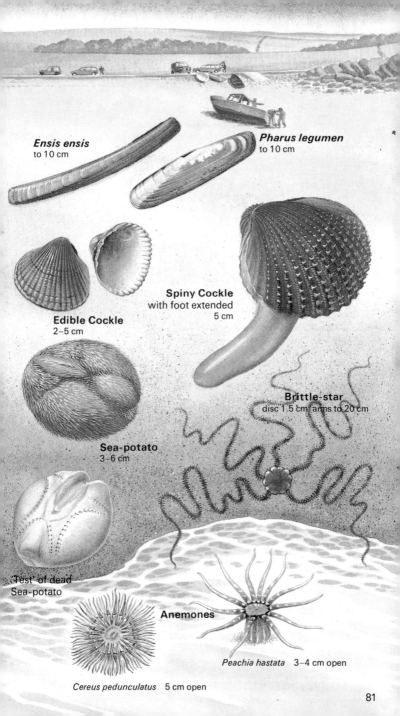

Ensis ensis
to 10 cm

Pharus legumen
to 10 cm

Spiny Cockle
with foot extended
5 cm

Edible Cockle
2–5 cm

Sea-potato
3–6 cm

Brittle-star
disc 1.5 cm; arms to 20 cm

'Test' of dead
Sea-potato

Anemones

Peachia hastata   3–4 cm open

Cereus pedunculatus   5 cm open

81

Sandy/Muddy Shore

Worms. The tubes of fanworms extend 30 cm down. Grains of silt and sand are captured from suspension in the water by rows of vibrating hairs on the tentacles which pass them onto the rim of the tube which is ready smeared with mucous-glue. Particles of food, caught in the same way, are deflected down into the worm's mouth. When the tide is out these worms withdraw into the security of the tube.

Thread-thin sticky tentacles of the **Stonemason Worm** quest over the sand surface, select grains of sand and carry them back to the glued rim by muscular contraction. The pale pink sticky tentacles searching on the surface for food fragments are all of *Amphitrite* ever to be outside its mucous tube 2–5 cm deep in the sand.

The **Lugworm** draws oxygenated water into its U-tube by muscular 'pumping'. The edge of the hole at the other end breaks up as this water is driven out, causing detritus to fall into the tube which the worm swallows. Food in it is digested and the unusable mass is excreted as casts out of the hole down which water is drawn.

Peacock Worm
to 9 cm above ground

Nephthys, *Phyllodoce*, the unsegmented (Nemertine) *Lineus* (the longest British animal) and *Tubulanus* are also deposit feeders, having expandable 'mouths' which indiscriminately engulf edible titbits. All these are commonly active in the surface layers of mud and muddy sand, the Nemertines particularly where a few stones have collected.

The predatory, omnivorous Nereids have hard chitinous jaws and teeth for breaking up what they catch. A large *virens* can draw blood from a finger.

Branchiomma vesiculosum
to 5 cm above ground

The lowest tides may expose a **Sea-mouse** which is a segmented worm (Annelid). The mat of hairs covering its back hides the 15 pairs of interlocking scales. This mat sieves off sand grains that would otherwise block the current into the respiratory space along the worm's back under the scales. The sea-mouse is another carrion crusher.

fans extended

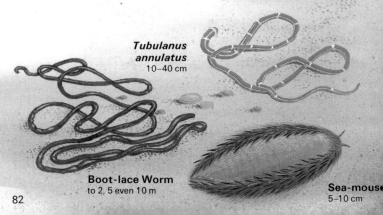

Tubulanus annulatus
10–40 cm

Boot-lace Worm
to 2, 5 even 10 m

Sea-mouse
5–10 cm

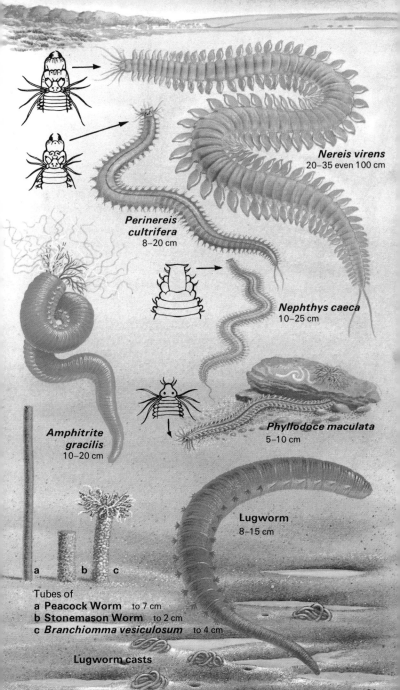

Nereis virens
20–35 even 100 cm

Perinereis cultrifera
8–20 cm

Nephthys caeca
10–25 cm

Amphitrite gracilis
10–20 cm

Phyllodoce maculata
5–10 cm

Lugworm
8–15 cm

Tubes of
a **Peacock Worm**   to 7 cm
b **Stonemason Worm**   to 2 cm
c *Branchiomma vesiculosum*   to 4 cm

Lugworm casts

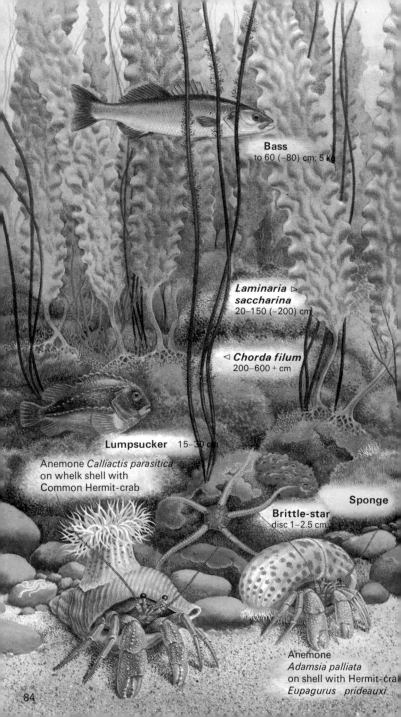

Bass
to 60 (–80) cm; 5 kg

Laminaria ▷
saccharina
20–150 (–200) cm

◁ *Chorda filum*
200–600 + cm

Lumpsucker   15–30 cm

Anemone *Calliactis parasitica*
on whelk shell with
Common Hermit-crab

Sponge

Brittle-star
disc 1–2.5 cm

Anemone
Adamsia palliata
on shell with Hermit-crab
Eupagurus   prideauxi

Sandy/Muddy Shore

When we visit the sand flats to dig bait or look for shells, all the seaweeds lie along the ground and nearly all the animals are safe within their burrows or under chance stones. Easy to forget that within six hours the water will be two, four or even six metres deep where we now stand. The flood tide renews the oxygen supply and carries in much of the food and many predatory fish and crabs that change the horizontal, hidden, low water time of resting to the vertical, busy high water time of movement, feeding and being fed on.

Rays, dogfish and flatfish (p.106, p.115) move in for crustacea, molluscs, worms and small fish. Amongst the round fish, **Bass** and **Lumpsuckers** typify those which eat shrimps, prawns, crabs, squids, sand-eels, etc. No wonder **Spider-crabs** attach a disguise of fragments of seaweed and sponge to body and legs.

The partnership between the **anemones** or **hydroids** on the shells within which live scavenging and suspension-feeding **Hermit-crabs** is sometimes of mutual benefit. The crab has additional protection from the anemone's stinging cells and the anemone has extra food as crumbs float up from the crab's meal. This 'symbiosis' (the shepherd and his dog) grades down to parasitism in which one partner takes to the other's disadvantage.

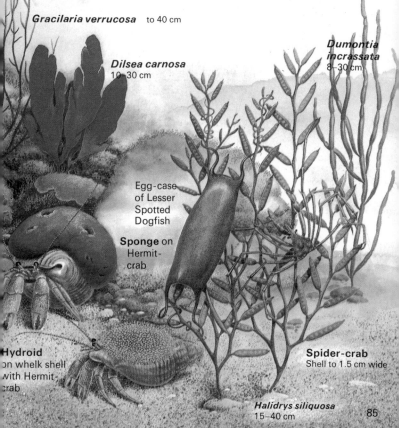

Gracilaria verrucosa   to 40 cm

Dilsea carnosa
10–30 cm

Dumontia incrassata
8–30 cm

Egg-case
of Lesser
Spotted
Dogfish

Sponge on
Hermit-
crab

Hydroid
on whelk shell
with Hermit-
crab

Spider-crab
Shell to 1.5 cm wide

Halidrys siliquosa
15–40 cm

85

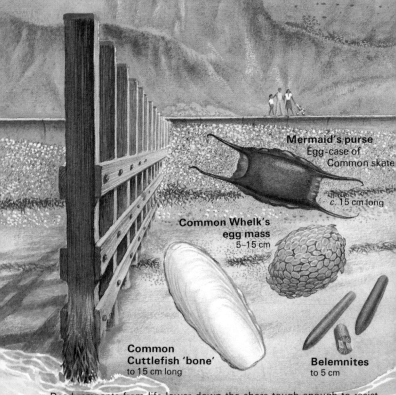

Mermaid's purse
Egg-case of
Common skate
c. 15 cm long

**Common Whelk's
egg mass**
5–15 cm

**Common
Cuttlefish 'bone'**
to 15 cm long

Belemnites
to 5 cm

Dead remnants from life lower down the shore tough enough to resist being smashed to pieces by waves accumulate along the strandline amongst man-made rubbish. Shells abound.

A coarse 'bath-sponge' is a **Common Whelk's** (p.76) **egg-mass**. When laid, the first sticky layer anchored the subsequent lump to a rock. The laying process lasts for several days. The masses from two females laying close together may fuse into one large lump.

In each capsule (cell) are about twelve fertile and a thousand 'nurse' eggs. By eating the nurses the newly hatched whelks grow that much larger and stronger before emerging through the capsule exit to the outside world. When all are hatched the empty mass breaks away and is cast ashore by tides and winds.

A single dogfish is hatched from the large yolked egg while the case (**mermaid's purse**) is still attached to seaweeds (p.85) and escapes from the slit at one end. Skates' cases have short stiff black points.

Cuttlefish (p.112) 'bones' are their internal shells. The **Common Cuttlefish's**, up to 10×30 cm, are abundant. Cigar-shaped stone 'bullets' are **Belemnites**, the fossil remains of relations to cuttlefish which flourished 100 million years ago. Found mostly from Weymouth to Flamborough.

The strandline never smells offensive because so many birds and **sandhoppers** scavenge so effectively.

The Strandline

Limpet
underside

Sandhopper
to 2 cm

Needle Shell
to 15 mm

Rissoa parva
to 70 mm

Auger Shell
to 6 cm

Wentletrap
to 4 cm

Pelican's
Foot
to 6 cm

Violet Sea-snail
to 3 cm

Tusk-shell
to 5 cm

*Arctica
islandica*
to 10 cm

Bonnet Limpet
c. 5 cm

87

Sand Dunes

The development of coastal sand dunes requires a supply of dry sand, wind to drive it ashore and a succession of vegetation to stabilise the accumulation. The surface of sand exposed at low tide, dried by wind and sun, will be blown before any wind over 15 kph. Dunes build only when onshore winds blow. The building is initiated by irregular obstructions presented by jetsam along the tideline and the few plants that can survive immersion by the highest tides that reach that level.

Morfa Harlech and Scolt Head are examples of dunes that have developed on the line of pre-existing shingle banks. But if the shingle lies obliquely to the building wind and if the sand supply is plentiful, the dunes will build at right angles to that wind uninfluenced by the alignment of the shingle. Although the dunes of Lancashire, the Moray Firth, on both sides of the Bristol Channel and on the East Anglian coast are large, they are entirely dwarfed by those in Holland and western France.

Marram grass (p.92) is the most influential biological agent in the fixing of dunes. The root system penetrates many feet and laterals develop successively as more and more sand is blown ashore. Marram can spread 3 metres laterally and a metre vertically every year.

As the dunes grow higher the wind speed at the top increases and may erode the seaward face faster than the sand can be replaced from the shore. So the dune system may move inland as much as 7 metres per year. On the other hand, where wind speeds are low and the supply of sand large, as one dune is stabilised by a carpet of plants a new dune will develop to seaward. Stability is also secured when the seeds of landward plants germinate in the autumn. The seedlings survive through the winter binding the sand surface and flower early enough to set seed again before the heat and drought of summer kills the parent plant. A combination of dead plants and rabbit droppings adds enough to the store of humus to hold additional moisture in the surface layers for the continued survival of perennial colonisers. The root system of the first colonisers runs deep enough to tap the water stored a few feet below the surface of sand (p.97).

The nature of the sand controls the vegetation that finally 'fixes' dunes. Where it is largely mineral grains, mostly of quartz, it is so acid that the accumulating humus remains so sour that heather and heath dominate the sward. Elsewhere sand containing lime-rich grains of ground-up shells neutralises the acidity, allowing a species-rich thicket to develop.

Much of the coastal crofting in western Scotland literally cannot survive without the shell-sand which blows over the ring of marram dunes onto sour inland peat. The sweetening is additionally encouraged by loads of wracks and oarweeds carried up from the strandline to be spread with the shell-sand. Winter flocks of Barnacle Geese (p.23) and the crofters' livestock add nutrients to the 'machair' turf upon which livelihoods depend.

Changes in wind dominance in historic times resulted in the 14th century overwhelming by sand of the town and port of Kenfig in Glamorgan. In Cornwall, in the 17th century, Gwithian Sands invaded Lelant church and, in the early 19th, St. Enodoc's church began to be ruined. Southport has been progressively extended seaward as new dunes are enclosed.

Sand dunes provide the opportunity, rare in Britain, to stand in one place and see before you every stage in a biological succession from bare ground through colonisation to stable thicket and even forest.

Shingle Banks

Driven before the wind, most waves have the power to move material shoreward from the seabed in proportion to their size and frequency. This power is substantially dissipated at the top of the shore as the water from each wave percolates down into the accumulated sand and stones. The bulk of the backwash is so much reduced that, although running downhill, it has only a fraction of the energy possessed by the oncoming swash. Consequently many shingle banks are footed by extensive sandy shores because, at those levels, the backwash can carry only sand while the forward swash drives all stones landward. The biggest stones are thrown to the top of the bank. Shingle banks are often called 'storm beaches', the highest levels being reached only during great gales – an exceptional one will throw boulders right over the beach, totally obstructing the road so often passing along its landward side.

On many coasts the effective winds drive the waves shoreward at an angle oblique to the line of the coast, but the backwash always returns to the sea at right angles with the result that the stones move sideways and the shingle beach is constantly being lengthened downwind. In the English Channel the prevailing SW winds lengthen the shingle eastwards but on the Suffolk coast, where the SW wind is equally prevailing, the effective wind is NE – its long approach (fetch) across the North Sea extends the shingle southwards. The many headlands, great and small, of an indented cliff coast effectively bar major pebble drifting.

Where the line of the coast abruptly changes direction, the shingle build may continue downwind as a spit. These spits deflect the flow of rivers, making them parallel to the shore – e.g. the Humber, Yar and Alde and many along the Channel. Strong winds persisting from an unusual direction may cause these spits to hook landward. The hooks are successively left behind as the effective wind reasserts its authority.

The movement of waves and tidal currents may also result in the building of shingle banks just offshore. The shape of the coast and persistence of the winds pile up material until a bank becomes an island. Rising and lengthening, this becomes connected with the mainland at one end or both, cutting off a lagoon on the landward side. The ten miles of Chesil Beach, Slapton, Loe Bar and Cemlyn are examples.

Where the shingle on these banks has a steep landward slope and the sea level at spring high tides is well above the lagoon level, so much water may percolate through the coarser shingle at the top of the bank that its flow displaces shingle landward. Where the conditions of size, angles and levels coincide, this percolation may initiate the cutting down of ravines into the bank through which the sea forces more and more shingle which fans out, reducing the lagoon to a flat shingle terrace. While the shingle is in motion, friction inhibits the development of vegetation.

Elsewhere, at Dungeness and Orfordness, the alignment of shingle ridges and hollows is evidence that wind and tide have progressively piled shingle onto both sides of a promontory. This seaward movement progresses still.

Some waves are 'destructive' and comb down the sand and shingle shores. They plunge vertically and may add their backwash energy to the backwash of the wave before. A flooding river may erode the landward side of a spit, and a combination of unexpected wind and spring-tide sea currents will gouge seaward faces. Much shingle is inherently unstable.

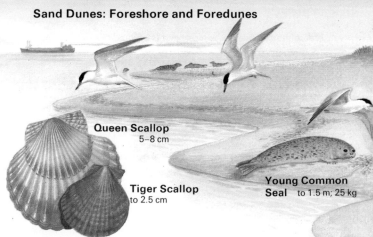

Queen Scallop
5–8 cm

Tiger Scallop
to 2.5 cm

Young Common Seal to 1.5 m; 25 kg

West Indian Beans

Entada gigas
to 5 cm

Macuna sp.
c. 3 cm

Sea-mats

Alcyonidium gelatinosum
6–15 cm

The **Common Seal** (in America, the Harbor Seal) is a cold water creature, living along coasts all round the North Pole, preferring inshore, shallow water. Although most often seen in Britain on the sandbanks of the east coast, they haul out on rock platforms in north Scotland. Males 2 m long, females 1.6 m; max. weight 100 kilos. They pup in midsummer and suckle for five weeks. Mating in September, the development of the foetus is delayed until midwinter.

Most terns arrive in April from W. African coasts. The **Arctic** makes the 16,000 km round trip to Antarctica annually. Unlike gulls, terns dive for their food. They often nest on just such a coast as this. The key to specific identities is the colour pattern of beaks and foreheads. They leave us for the south in early autumn.

About a dozen kinds of seeds which fall from plants overhanging the sea in tropical America have outer skins tough enough to continue to buoy them for the two years it takes to drift on the Gulf Stream as far as our coasts, there to be thrown ashore by waves.

Dead-man's Fingers is a soft coral, remotely related to sea anemones. ***Flustra foliacea*** is a sea-mat (p.64). Both live below low water. Only their 'skeletons' are cast ashore.

Flustra foliacea
6–15 cm

Roseate Tern

Arctic Tern

l. 38 cm, s. 75 cm

l. 35 cm, s. 80 cm

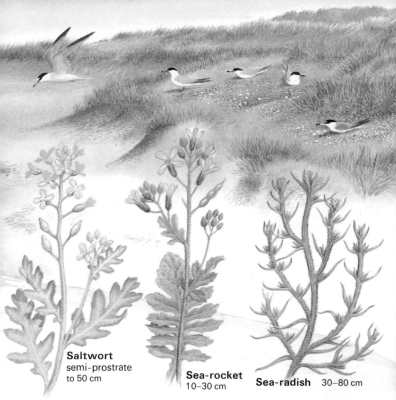

Saltwort
semi-prostrate
to 50 cm

Sea-rocket
10–30 cm

Sea-radish 30–80 cm

Refuse rotting along the tideline provides humus enough for the most seaward-flowering plant colonists to survive on ground not constantly eroded by wind or waves. On warm days, when the tide is out, the refuse and plants in turn arrest the inland progress of dried sand drifting landward from the sandy shore below. So the foredunes build and are stabilised by the dense root systems of Sand Couch-grass. *Agropyron juncei-forme*, which may grow a metre tall. Only those plants which can tolerate total immersion in seawater at the highest spring tides survive on the foreshore. A great gale may completely destroy the community. While **Sea-rocket**, **Sea-radish** and **Saltwort** are common, Sea-beet and Sea-sandwort (p.95) often grow there too. Seedlings of many higher dune and shingle species may survive at this level long enough to flower.

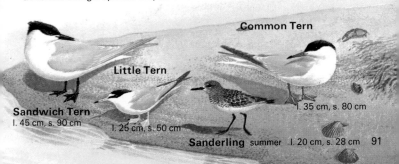

Common Tern

Little Tern

Sandwich Tern
l. 45 cm, s. 90 cm

l. 25 cm, s. 50 cm

l. 35 cm, s. 80 cm

Sanderling summer l. 20 cm, s. 28 cm 91

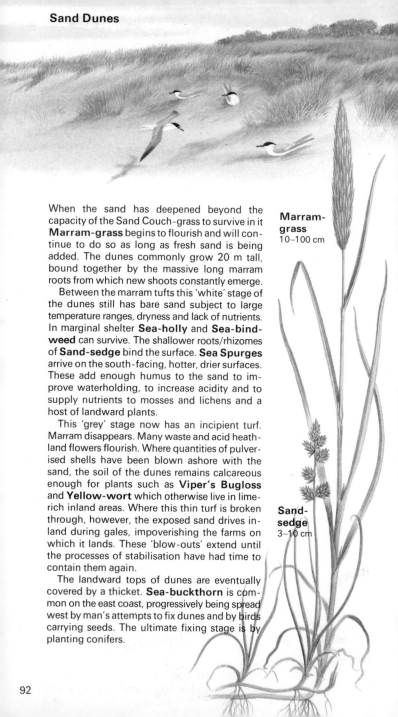

When the sand has deepened beyond the capacity of the Sand Couch-grass to survive in it **Marram-grass** begins to flourish and will continue to do so as long as fresh sand is being added. The dunes commonly grow 20 m tall, bound together by the massive long marram roots from which new shoots constantly emerge.

Between the marram tufts this 'white' stage of the dunes still has bare sand subject to large temperature ranges, dryness and lack of nutrients. In marginal shelter **Sea-holly** and **Sea-bindweed** can survive. The shallower roots/rhizomes of **Sand-sedge** bind the surface. **Sea Spurges** arrive on the south-facing, hotter, drier surfaces. These add enough humus to the sand to improve waterholding, to increase acidity and to supply nutrients to mosses and lichens and a host of landward plants.

This 'grey' stage now has an incipient turf. Marram disappears. Many waste and acid heathland flowers flourish. Where quantities of pulverised shells have been blown ashore with the sand, the soil of the dunes remains calcareous enough for plants such as **Viper's Bugloss** and **Yellow-wort** which otherwise live in lime-rich inland areas. Where this thin turf is broken through, however, the exposed sand drives inland during gales, impoverishing the farms on which it lands. These 'blow-outs' extend until the processes of stabilisation have had time to contain them again.

The landward tops of dunes are eventually covered by a thicket. **Sea-buckthorn** is common on the east coast, progressively being spread west by man's attempts to fix dunes and by birds carrying seeds. The ultimate fixing stage is by planting conifers.

Marram-grass
10–100 cm

Sand-sedge
3–10 cm

Yellow-wort
15–45 cm

Sea-buckthorn
50–300 cm

Viper's Bugloss
10–80 cm

Sea-bindweed
prostrate; to 60 cm long

Portland Spurge
5–30 cm

Sea-holly
10–30 cm

Sea-spurge
15–35 cm

Shingle Bank: Flowers and Waders

Sea-sandwort, a typical fore dune colonist (p.91), and **Sea-campion**, typical of rocky cliffs, are both common on shingle. Their low habit, their ability to withstand spray, their extensive root systems binding loose shingle mixed with sand and their issue of aerial roots when buried by stones make them early colonists.

Sea-beet and several species of **Orache** are quite at home where sand drifts up against a shingle bank. The beet is the plant from which beetroots, mangolds and sugar-beet have all been derived. Persian gardeners round the Mediterranean started the selective breeding some 2,000 years ago. Its leaves, boiled for about five minutes and served with a dollop of butter, are much nicer than spinach. Orache is not so good.

Sea-mayweed is particularly abundant in west Scotland and Ireland.

Where shingle banks grade off into the mud of a saltmarsh, perhaps at the mouth of an estuary, waders may congregate when the flood tide has driven them from their feeding grounds. The secret of seeing them well is to settle down with the sun behind you. A broken fish basket and other large jetsam provide adequate cover. Then just wait quietly for them to come to you. I once had eleven species, all at one time, within thirty yards of me. He who restlessly moves after them sees almost nothing but specks in the middle distance.

In a spot like this some of the saltmarsh plants survive amongst the stones.

Bar-tailed Godwit
l. 38 cm, s. 47 cm

Curlew
l. 55 cm, s. 67 cm

Grey Plover
l. 28 cm, s. 44 cm

Turnstone l. 23 cm, s. c. 35 cm

Whimbrel
l. 41 cm, s. 55 cm

Dunlin
l. 18 cm, s. 25 cm

Ringed Plover
l. 19 cm, s. 27 cm

Sanderling
l. 20 cm, s. 25 cm

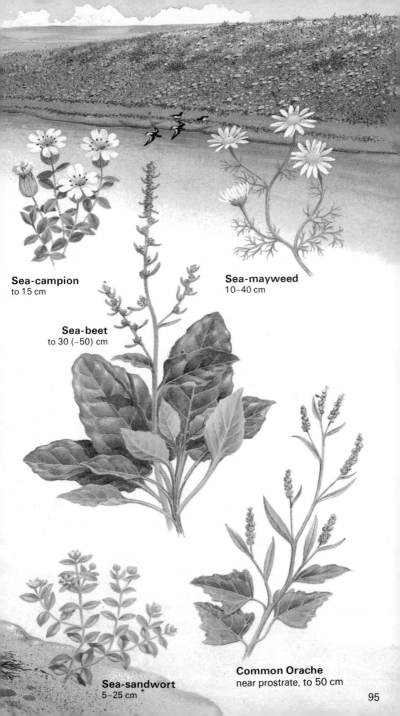

Sea-campion
to 15 cm

Sea-mayweed
10–40 cm

Sea-beet
to 30 (–50) cm

Common Orache
near prostrate, to 50 cm

Sea-sandwort
5–25 cm

95

Shingle Bank: Flowers

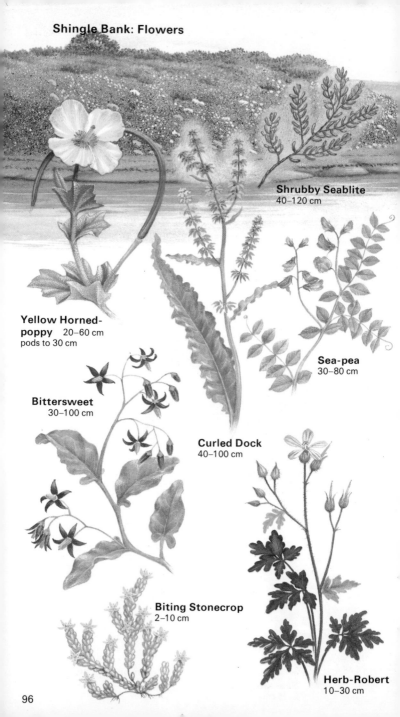

Shrubby Seablite 40–120 cm

Yellow Horned-poppy 20–60 cm
pods to 30 cm

Sea-pea 30–80 cm

Bittersweet 30–100 cm

Curled Dock 40–100 cm

Biting Stonecrop 2–10 cm

Herb-Robert 10–30 cm

The friction of stones rubbing together inhibits the growth of plants. Plant life is continuous only on shingle that is stable and permanently out of reach of the tide. The first humus essential for its establishment derives from the rotting of refuse blown up or thrown up during gales.

Fresh water abounds in shingle. Rain percolates deep, and the absence of soil inhibits evaporation by capillary action when the top layers of stones quickly warm up. This causes air to be squeezed out of those top layers by expansion. Somewhat cooler, damper air then percolates in through the lower layers of the bank from which moisture condenses and is added to the water-stock when the shingle chills in the evening. The next day the air from which the moisture condensed is drawn out of the top by warming and the cycle is repeated. In addition, dew drips down from the cold night surface.

The shingle plants have roots long enough to reach down to this fresh water which, being lighter, floats on the salt lower down. Much the same circulation makes water available in sand-dunes (p.88). The leaves and flowering stems of **Curled Docks** die as soon as the seeds ripen but retain strength to stay in situ over winter, thereby sheltering the new growth against excessive salt spray from winter gales. The slow lichens obviously require stability.

Stonechat
l. 12 cm, s. 13 cm

Thick hairs on the **Yellow Horned-poppy** leaves protect them from spray. The erect flower stalks survive only in the quiet of summer. Nitrogen fixed by the **Sea-pea**, found on Suffolk and Sussex beaches, is a nutrient for other plants. **Bittersweet** and **Herb Robert** indicate shingle stability; but no plant binds the surface more effectively than **Shrubby Seablite**.

Stonechats flick their tails on the tiptop of coastal bushes. **Wheatears** live where there are no bushes; like rabbits, their white rumps catch the eye.

Wheatear
l. 16 cm,
s. 23 cm

97

Saltmarsh: Origin and Building

A saltmarsh is likely to develop wherever a flat or muddy area is completely sheltered from the waves behind a shingle bank or sand bar or along the muddy sides of the lowest reaches of streams and rivers. Large ones are by the Solway and the Wash and in the estuaries of the Thames, Humber and Dovey. Fragments occur in a myriad quiet corners round the coast.

They are all built from silt held in suspension by moving water. The river brings its load downstream. The flood tide hastens with its load upstream. Where the two meet, particularly around high tide, both movements are so slowed that some of the silt falls to the ground. Deposition is increased where a barrier of stones or snagged refuse or even chance irregularities of surface texture additionally decelerate water movement.

In this way areas build up to a height at which green seaweeds or eelgrass (p.112) can establish themselves. This further slows water movement which in turn hastens deposition. Muddy mounds begin to stand out above the low tide expanse. When these are high enough to be left uncovered for three consecutive days by the high water level of late summer neap tides, the waterborne seeds of Glasswort have the time they need to attach themselves by rooting. Seeds which fall on the mud too low down to be undisturbed for three days are scoured out before they can secure themselves.

The Glasswort slows down the water still more. Even the stiff, dead stalks in winter are an effective barrier. The mud builds up to a level at which other plants can colonise it. The sequence varies somewhat from place to place; but all of them are necessarily true halophytes (p.45).

The original low mounds grow still larger. Before long they may coalesce. By doing so they start to restrict the horizontal movement of the tide to the gaps between the mounds. Being restricted, the thrust of the water is increased, notably at the earlier stage of the ebb when the volume spread over all the marsh is drawn down through comparatively narrow channels. These channels are progressively scoured deeper and steeper into the marsh level.

The edge of these deeper channels gives the sharper drainage which

Sea-purslane (p.101) prefers. The veritable thicket of interlocking stems substantially slows down water movement, especially where the red seaweed *Bostrichia* (p.101) attaches itself to them. As the edges of the drainage channels build up higher again, a level is reached at which sufficiently few tides cover the ground to allow more flowering plants to survive. Sea-pinks and Sea-lavender colonise and then force out the Sea-purslane. At this stage we have the saltmarsh turf lonely and windswept in winter but beautiful in the flowers of summer.

Quite often scouring erosion undercuts and then collapses parts of the steep sides of the drainage channels. The mattresses of Sea-purslane that dominated both edges now lock together to complete the cut-off of the upper length of the channel which rapidly fills with silt, to form the drainage 'pan' so common in the Sea-pink and Sea-lavender turf.

These pans are fiercely inhospitable. Left full of salt-water by the last tide to reach them before their neap isolation, evaporation increases the salinity in hot weather until the pool is dry, leaving crystalline salt shining on the mud. In rainy weather all salt may be quickly washed out: the previously supersaline pool now has a salinity down to $1°/oo$ (p.12). The large day–night and summer–winter temperature ranges sharpen the salinity rigours. Only the tiny snail *Hydrobia* and the woodlouse relation *Sphaeroma* (p.108) can live in that mud. Shrimps and gobies survive as long as there is water, no matter what the salinity. All are eaten by waders.

Sea Meadow-grass is the first to colonise the pan mud. Where growth from the edges meets across the middle the linear pan is subdivided. The rate of silt accretion is accelerated and the erstwhile channel is incorporated into the Sea-pink turf. Meanwhile, bank collapse elsewhere has started the cycle again: the stages are clear to see on most marshes. On close inspection the turf is found to be inhabited by huge numbers of little beetles, mites and sandhoppers, all of which are food for birds.

If sea level was constant (which it never is) about two centuries are needed to complete the saltmarsh development from the first Glasswort to the final Sea-rush (p.105).

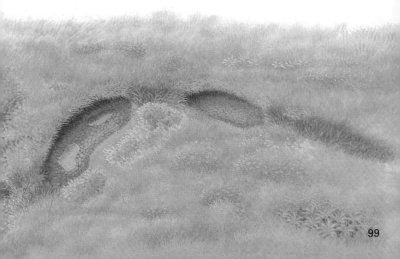

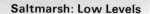

Saltmarsh: Low Levels

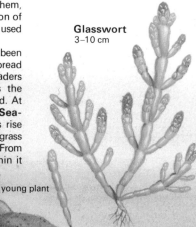

That plants at the lowest levels of saltmarshes truly flower in July and August is not readily apparent. They belong to the Goosefoot family. The short segments towards the ends of the stem and branches of **Glasswort**, alias Marsh Samphire, produces minute flowers in pits at the nodes. The **Seablite** has small green flowers recognisable through a lens but often hidden by the leaves.

Identifying the several species of **Glasswort** is so technical that we are sticking here to the generic shape. Glasswort occupies the lowest zone wherever the substrate is firm enough for the roots to hold (p.98). The scale-like leaves are adapted to conserve fresh water which the plant can separate from the wholly salt environment in which it lives. Delicious in sandwiches, Glasswort also makes a good pickle. Its ashes contain impure carbonate of soda which was mixed with sand in primitive glass-making.

Annual Seablite, next above the Glasswort, particularly where sand is mixed with mud, also occurs up to the Sea-lavender zone.

Cord-grass, a cross between the native *Spartina maritima* and the American *S. alterniflora*, has all the vigour of a mongrel. It was first noticed in Southampton Water in 1870 and has now spread up the east and west coasts and to Ireland. Flourishing particularly in loose wet mud, it totally dominates the lower zones of many drainage channels. The speed with which the marsh landscape is transformed after its first arrival is extraordinary. The 1 m and more stems sprouting from thick tussocks notably slow water movement through them, with the resulting rapid deposition of mud. Indeed, Cord-grass is much used in land reclamation.

Glasswort
3–10 cm

In some marshes Glasswort has been almost eliminated by the lower spread of Cord-grass. As it spreads waders and ducks become scarcer as the source of their food is destroyed. At its upper edge it merges into the **Sea-purslane** (p.99). As the levels rise the mud becomes drier, the Cord-grass weakens and is finally eliminated. From its first settlement it carries within it the cause of its own destruction.

young plant

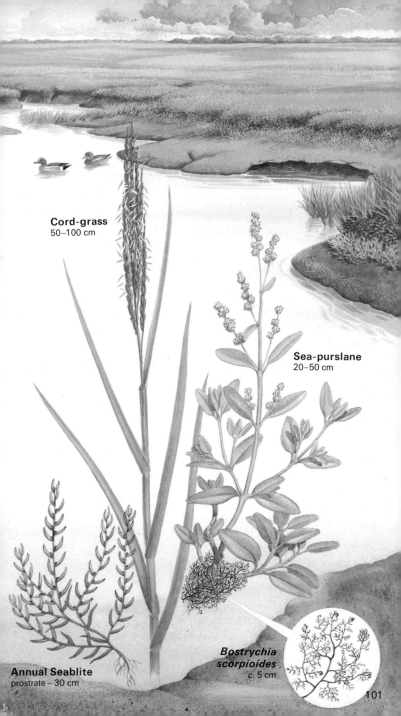

Cord-grass
50–100 cm

Sea-purslane
20–50 cm

Annual Seablite
prostrate – 30 cm

Bostrychia scorpioides
c. 5 cm

101

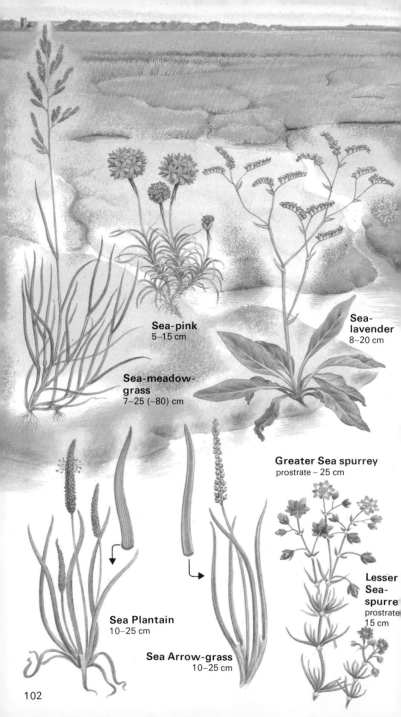

Sea-pink
5–15 cm

Sea-
lavender
8–20 cm

Sea-meadow-
grass
7–25 (–80) cm

Greater Sea spurrey
prostrate – 25 cm

Lesser
Sea-
spurre
prostrate
15 cm

Sea Plantain
10–25 cm

Sea Arrow-grass
10–25 cm

Sea-aster
15–50 (–100) cm

These flowers are all common in the low and middle levels of a saltmarsh which the sea does not reach during neap weeks throughout the year. The proportions and precise levels vary greatly from marsh to marsh.

Where the ground is more sand than mud the Sea Meadow-grass may dominate a zone just above the Glasswort. Its lateral growths root down as well as shooting up. A turf forms quickly; water movement is slowed. So the level of the ground rises high enough for Sea-aster to colonise the Sea Meadow-grass turf. This happens particularly on the east coast. The Sea-aster flowers late enough to justify the local name Michaelmas Daisy. However garden Michaelmas Daisies largely derive from American asters. By its height and bulk Sea-aster obstructs water movement further; ground level rises enough for Sea-lavender and Sea-pink to flourish.

The Sea-pink is the same beautiful plant as lives on the cliffs. All the middle level of the saltmarsh is coloured by it in May and June, followed by Sea-lavender, blue-purple in high summer. These hazes of colour, picked out by the other flowers, embody the essence of the word 'saltings'.

Scurvy-grass is a close relation to Watercress and not a grass at all. Rich in vitamin-C, it was used to combat scurvy long before becoming an essential medicine on those sailing voyages from the 16th century onwards. The taste is revolting. Crews must have cheered when lime juice replaced it.

Sea-Plaintain and Spurrey are others that also thrive in the splash zone of rocky shores (p.44).

Common Scurvy-grass
5–25 cm

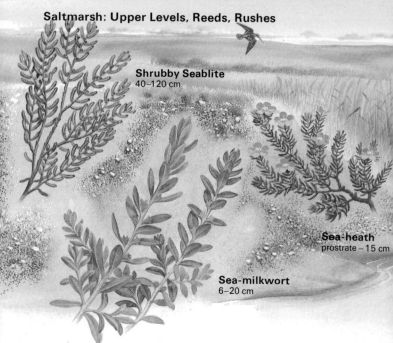

Shrubby Seablite
40–120 cm

Sea-heath
prostrate – 15 cm

Sea-milkwort
6–20 cm

At the top of the saltmarsh, especially where freshwater drains off the higher ground beyond, a zone of rushes often grows. **Sea-rush** and **Saltmarsh Rush** may occur alone or mixed together where seawater reaches for only an hour or two each month. Their dense growth casts deep shade and their roots also inhibit the survival of the flowering plants of the middle zones. So damp mud appears amongst the stems which shelter snipe and water-rail in winter.

Where the freshwater element is fed by a stream, no matter how small, **Sea Club-rush** will mix with the other rushes, and the most seaward of the large **Common Reeds** will survive down to where the high water of spring tides penetrates. The short invasions of salt are quickly washed out by the ever-flowing fresh stream. Common Reed is really a grass and is the epitome of the idea of freshwater reedbeds.

Only just beyond the reach of the spring high tides, the first Sallow bushes establish themselves in the reedbed. Higher still, isolated bushes become a thicket. The first Alder seedlings are the next in the succession that leads on to deciduous forests – a succession that started when Glasswort established itself in the low tide mud.

Elsewhere the saltmarsh may have been established at the foot of a shingle bank. Along south and east coasts the junction between the two habitats is likely to be marked by the Mediterranean plants **Shrubby Seablite** and **Sea-heath**. Among the plants of the drier, shingly top edges of the saltmarsh **Sea-milkwort** is often abundant. The beauty of its flowers is fully revealed only to those who look carefully through a handlens.

Snipe

Water-rail

**Saltmarsh
Rush**
10–30 cm

Sea-rush
30–80 cm

Sea Club-rush
50–90 cm

Common Reed
2–3 cm

105

Sea-trout
20–50 (–100 c

Grey Mullet
15–50 cm

Sprat
10–15 cm

Plaice
8–30 cm

Flounder
8–15 cm

Dab
8–15 cm

The biological problem confronting all organisms living in an estuary is how to survive the range of salinity from fresh to fully marine water. Pure water can pass through animal or plant membranes, including those enclosing individual cells, but salts dissolved in water cannot. If two solutions of different strengths are separated by such a membrane, water passes from the weaker through the membrane to dilute the stronger until the two are of equal strength. This process is called osmosis.

During the flood tide, when the salinity of an estuary increases, water will pass out of the bodies of the animals that were in brackish solutions, leaving them with excess salt they must immediately get rid of. On the ebb tide, on the other hand, as the fresh river water progressively dominates the sea, extra water will continue to pass into those animals with a higher salt content. They would burst unless they pump it out.

Because salt water is heavier than fresh, the flood tide thrusts upstream along the bottom of the channel, while the fresh still runs downstream on top. The vertical salinity range at any one place fluctuates with the state of the tide and complicates the variations caused by the horizontal ebb and flow.

Common Goby
5–10 cm

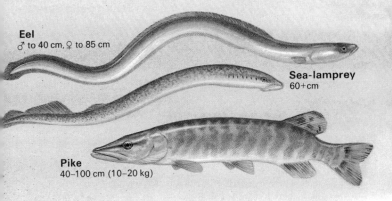

Eel
♂ to 40 cm, ♀ to 85 cm

Sea-lamprey
60+ cm

Pike
40–100 cm (10–20 kg)

Animals' protective mechanisms are various. The bodies of some soft creatures such as worms may simply get bigger and smaller as the tide falls and rises. This option is not open to fish.

To survive in an estuary a fish expels unwanted salt through its gills and has kidneys that produce urine in balancing quantities. The concentration of salt in the blood of marine fish is always somewhat lower than in the seawater itself. So **Dabs** and **Plaice** are in no difficulty in the lower reaches of estuaries as they push up for worms and mysids. The **Flounder** is the estuarine fish *par excellence*. It can adjust salt 'tensions' in its blood from over 5 in the sea to only 1½ in brackish water. So its food ranges from freshwater insects to shrimps, *Nereis* and *Corophium*.

The **Common Goby** is another abundant estuarine resident, surviving even in pools of extreme salinity range (p.99).

As they migrate upstream **Salmon** and **Sea-trout** balance external lower salinity by increasing their internal urine volume a hundredfold.

Young **Mullet** flourish upstream to 3°/∘∘ salt but go down to the sea to spawn.

Sprats penetrate estuaries only in summer when the freshwater run off is minimal. Their pursuit by mackerel peters out when low salinity bars the unadapted predator.

In the Baltic **Pike** tolerate salt water to where herring tolerate fresh: so pike eat herring there.

The number of boney plates on the sides of the **Three-spined Stickle-back** decreases from 20–30 on those living in freshwater to 4–5 in brackish. How this controls salt tensions nobody knows.

Sea-lampreys come a short way upstream to spawn and then they die. The larvae go back to sea, to attach themselves to Cod, Haddock, Salmon, etc. They mature in a year or two and return upstream to spawn, laying up to 200,000 eggs, before dying.

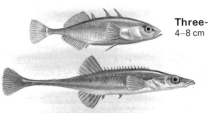

Three-spined Stickleback
4–8 cm

Fifteen-spined Stickleback
8–12 (–20) cm

Far fewer species of animals live in fresh water than live in the sea. Even so they greatly outnumber those who live only in estuaries. Most of these are bound by salinity tolerances; just how tightly is shown by three closely related snails. The freshwater *Potamopyrgus jenkinsi* survives into 15°/oo sea water (p.12). *Hydrobia ventrosa* lives in brackish creeks at 6–20°/oo. The numbers of *H. ulvae* on the midtidal mud, 10–33 +°/oo, far exceed 10,000 per sq. m.

Sandhoppers (Amphipods) are common, each species in its own salinity range, up to the Freshwater Shrimp (not a shrimp!) in only fresh water. Of all the barnacles only *Balanus improvisus* survives into 3°/oo. The flatworm *Procerodes* is under stones in the mouth of fresh streams that are only occasionally reached by salt water. While *Sphaeroma* and *Palae-monetes* flourish in estuarine/saltmarsh pools, neither can live on the seashore.

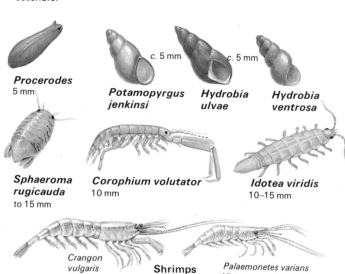

Procerodes
5 mm

c. 5 mm

c. 5 mm

Potamopyrgus jenkinsi

Hydrobia ulvae

Hydrobia ventrosa

Sphaeroma rugicauda
to 15 mm

Corophium volutator
10 mm

Idotea viridis
10–15 mm

Crangon vulgaris
2–5 cm

Shrimps

Palaemonetes varians
15 mm

Sandhopper
2 cm

Balanus improvisus
2 cm

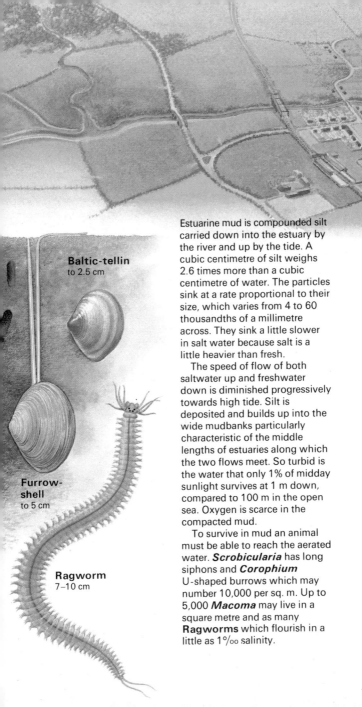

Baltic-tellin
to 2.5 cm

Furrow-shell
to 5 cm

Ragworm
7–10 cm

Estuarine mud is compounded silt carried down into the estuary by the river and up by the tide. A cubic centimetre of silt weighs 2.6 times more than a cubic centimetre of water. The particles sink at a rate proportional to their size, which varies from 4 to 60 thousandths of a millimetre across. They sink a little slower in salt water because salt is a little heavier than fresh.

The speed of flow of both saltwater up and freshwater down is diminished progressively towards high tide. Silt is deposited and builds up into the wide mudbanks particularly characteristic of the middle lengths of estuaries along which the two flows meet. So turbid is the water that only 1% of midday sunlight survives at 1 m down, compared to 100 m in the open sea. Oxygen is scarce in the compacted mud.

To survive in mud an animal must be able to reach the aerated water. **Scrobicularia** has long siphons and **Corophium** U-shaped burrows which may number 10,000 per sq. m. Up to 5,000 **Macoma** may live in a square metre and as many **Ragworms** which flourish in a little as 1°/oo salinity.

Estuaries: Ducks and Waders

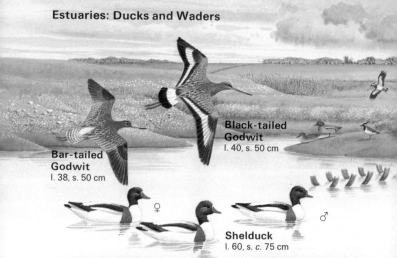

Black-tailed Godwit
l. 40, s. 50 cm

Bar-tailed Godwit
l. 38, s. 50 cm

Shelduck
l. 60, s. *c.* 75 cm

The mass of food available on saltmarshes and in estuaries is exploited by many birds. The open landscape secures them against surprise. Ducks and waders congregate in winter while others pass through on their spring and autumn migrations. Ours is a spring picture, with a selection of birds in breeding plumage, mostly ready to fly on to northern latitudes. The substantial differences between summer and winter plumages, most of all in waders, may puzzle inexperienced observers.

The long legs and beak of the **Heron** enable him to catch fish and crabs in relatively deep water. Of the surface feeders, the **Shelduck**'s mainstay is the hydrobid snails, with *Corophium* and *Nereis* (p.109). **Wigeon** particularly relish eel-grass (p.112); **Teal** go for glasswort and those little snails. The wide range of **Mallard** food includes eel-grass and small molluscs. **Goldeneye** dive for shrimps and sandhoppers, *Idotea*, small crabs and molluscs. So does the **Little Grebe** (Dabchick) which also catches small fish.

The waders are beautifully adapted to exploit all the opportunities. The long beaks of Curlew and **godwits** reach down for nereids and lugworms. **Redshank** and **Greenshank** get worms and up to 40,000 *Corophium* each per day. The small **plovers**, **Dunlin** and **Curlew-sandpiper** have beaks stout enough, but short, to cope with almost anything on or within 3–4 cm of the surface. A **Knot** takes over 700 *Macoma* daily.

The heavy beaks of Oystercatchers enable them to specialise on small cockles or mussels, so thinning the population in the mud for others to grow on to a size that man can harvest.

The gulls, so abundant in estuaries, are carnivores and scavengers, rivalled only by man in the variety of their diet.

l.28, s *c.* 43 cm

l. 28, s.*c.* 45 cm

Grey Plover

Teal

Golden Plover

Knot
l. 25, s. *c.* 38 cm

l. 35, s.*c.* 40 cm

Heron
l. 90, s. *c.* 100 cm

Wigeon
l. 46, s. *c.* 57 cm

♀ ♂ ♂

Mallard
l. 58, s. *c.* 60 cm

♀

♀

Goldeneye
l. 46, s. *c.* 50 cm

♂

Greenshank
l. 31, s. *c.* 43 cm

Little Grebe
l. 27, s. *c.* 26 cm

Redshank
l. 28, s. *c.* 38 cm

Dunlin

summer

Dunlin
l. 18, s. *c.* 27 cm

winter

summer

Curlew-sandpiper
l. 19, s. *c.* 30 cm

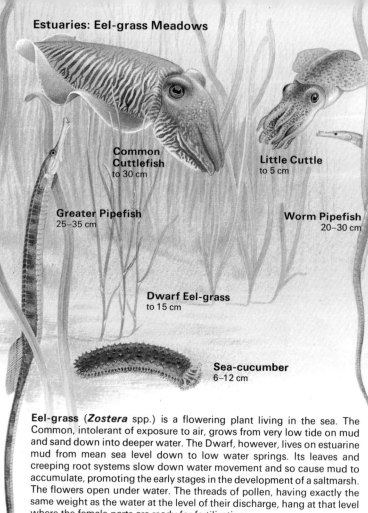

Common Cuttlefish
to 30 cm

Little Cuttle
to 5 cm

Greater Pipefish
25–35 cm

Worm Pipefish
20–30 cm

Dwarf Eel-grass
to 15 cm

Sea-cucumber
6–12 cm

Burrowing Shrimp
to 3 cm

Eel-grass (*Zostera* spp.) is a flowering plant living in the sea. The Common, intolerant of exposure to air, grows from very low tide on mud and sand down into deeper water. The Dwarf, however, lives on estuarine mud from mean sea level down to low water springs. Its leaves and creeping root systems slow down water movement and so cause mud to accumulate, promoting the early stages in the development of a saltmarsh. The flowers open under water. The threads of pollen, having exactly the same weight as the water at the level of their discharge, hang at that level where the female parts are ready for fertilisation.

In the 1930s a strange disease greatly reduced the extent and density of the Common's populations. This led to the collapse of some stabilised mudbanks and the renewal of estuarine erosion. Recovery has been intermittent and slow. The Dwarf was not affected.

Common Eel-grass meadows have an unlikely group of animals associated with them. The protective shape of **Pipefish** does not save them from herons. The males carry the fertilised eggs on their undersides until they hatch in midsummer. Pairs of **Burrowing Shrimps** inhabit permanent burrows amongst eel-grass so low that they are rarely exposed. At that lowest level the **Sea-cucumber** occurs in the southwest.

Cuttlefish have 'bones' (p.86) filled with gas, giving buoyancy equal to their weight. So, when not swimming, they hang effortlessly in the water protected from predators by an upper surface that has three layers of colour cells – the top, bright yellow; middle, orange-red; the lowest, red-brown or darker. Muscular movements reshape these cells to emit varying disruptive or terrorising shades and patterns. As a last resort, a cloud of 'ink', emitted through the anus, covers escape from a hungry conger. They eat shrimps, small crabs, etc.

Opossum Shrimps (Mysids) are hugely common, hanging vertically in coastal waters, rock pools and amongst eel-grass. They can change colour as dark night follows light day and, in accord with their background, from almost transparent in open water to grey-brown in estuaries where multitudes penetrate to a salinity as low as 3°/oo. By backward flicks they escape hungry plaice and sticklebacks, etc. Their food is filtered and scavenged from the water.

The sea-slug *Alderia*, on filamentous green seaweeds growing with eel-grass, survives into salinities down to 5°/oo. *Akera* lives on eel-grass mud. It lays 18,000 eggs in one mass.

The *Cantharidus* Topshell and both *Idotea*s eat the eel-grass and are eaten by fish and waders.

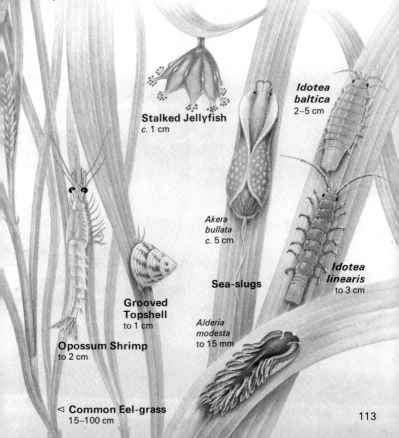

Idotea baltica
2–5 cm

Stalked Jellyfish
c. 1 cm

Akera bullata
c. 5 cm

Idotea linearis
to 3 cm

Sea-slugs

Grooved Topshell
to 1 cm

Alderia modesta
to 15 mm

Opossum Shrimp
to 2 cm

◁ **Common Eel-grass**
15–100 cm

Cormorants have yet to evolve feathers which do not waterlog. So, from time to time, wings are spread and gently flapped to dry them out again. The white thigh-patch is only breeding plumage.

imm.

adult in summer

Cormorant
l. 90, s. 150 cm

Black-headed Gull
l. 40, s. 90 cm

imm.

summer

winter

114

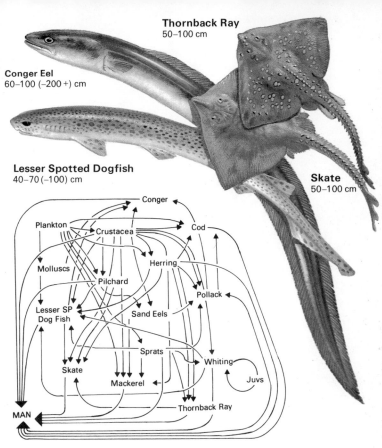

Thornback Ray
50–100 cm

Conger Eel
60–100 (–200 +) cm

Lesser Spotted Dogfish
40–70 (–100) cm

Skate
50–100 cm

Conger
Plankton
Crustacea
Cod
Molluscs
Herring
Pilchard
Pollack
Lesser SP
Dog Fish
Sand Eels
Sprats
Whiting
Skate
Mackerel
Juvs
MAN
Thornback Ray

A fraction of a foodweb supporting the smallest fishing quay.

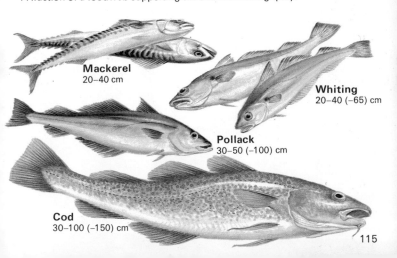

Mackerel
20–40 cm

Whiting
20–40 (–65) cm

Pollack
30–50 (–100) cm

Cod
30–100 (–150) cm

115

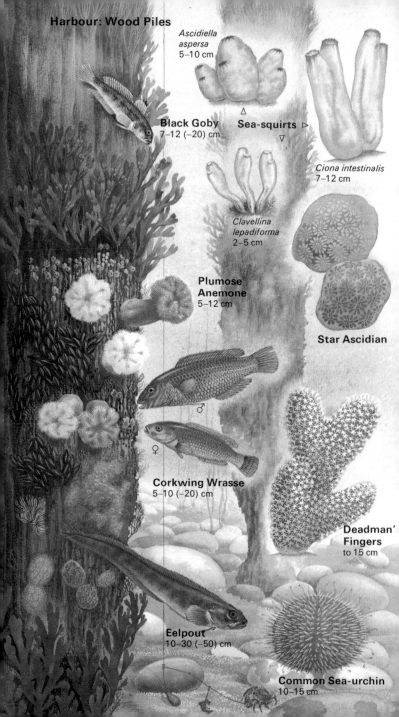

Harbour: Wood Piles

Ascidiella aspersa 5–10 cm

Black Goby 7–12 (–20) cm

Sea-squirts ▷

Ciona intestinalis 7–12 cm

Clavellina lepadiforma 2–5 cm

Plumose Anemone 5–12 cm

Star Ascidian

Corkwing Wrasse 5–10 (–20) cm

♂

♀

Deadman' Fingers to 15 cm

Eelpout 10–30 (–50) cm

Common Sea-urchin 10–15 cm

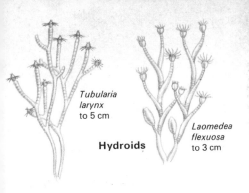

Tubularia
larynx
to 5 cm

Laomedea
flexuosa
to 3 cm

Hydroids

Kirchenpaueria
pinnata
to 12 cm

Piles which drive down through deep, unpolluted, quiet, tidal water into a stoney-rocky bottom offer fruitful anchorage to layers of plants and animals which develop to a size and rounded, fleshy maturity denied to them by wave action where they normally live. Where a decking shades them from desiccation they can live at a higher tidal level than elsewhere.

Populations on concrete and steel are less varied than those on wood where the surface, pitted by the gribble borings, gives an easier, if false, security of foothold.

The **Gribble** is an isopod. The female's jaws rasp hollows from MSL downwards in the softer grains from which a tunnel gently slopes. The amphipod *Chelura* enlarges the hollow. As the female gribble progresses she cuts a series of shafts through to the surface for water/respiration and food. Her digestive arrangements do not include the enzyme that breaks down wood cellulose into soluble sugars; so she cannot eat the 'sawdust' she cuts.

When the tunnel is 25 mm long the male, who lives behind the female in the tunnel doing none of the work, copulates with her. Eggs produce 25–30 young about 1 mm long who bore side galleries; the gribble infestation builds to some 50 per sq cm and the timber surface is destroyed. The next layer is then attacked until the pile loses structural strength. Adults swim or crawl to new piles in winter/spring. They even attack underwater cables. The much bigger galleries cut by the shipworm (p.63) accelerate the destruction.

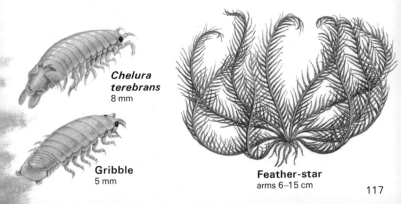

*Chelura
terebrans*
8 mm

Gribble
5 mm

Feather-star
arms 6–15 cm

Wind speed: Beaufort Scale

In 1805 Admiral Beaufort RN produced the scale of wind speed at sea which is still universally used. A knot is a nautical mile (6080ft) (= 1 minute of latitude on the equator) per hour.

Beaufort Scale no	Speed in knots	Descriptive terms	State of sea	Management of a 10 metre Sailing boat	Motor boat
0	0–1	calm	Like a mirror		
1	1–3	light air	Ripples like scales; no foam		
2	4–6	light breeze	Small wavelets do not break	Heeling 5–10° light helm	Small rolling with beam se
3	7–10	gentle breeze	Large wavelets; crests begin to break		
4	11–16	moderate breeze	Small waves; fairly frequent white horses	Heeling 15–20°. Spray developing. Use smaller headsail	Helmsman begins to study seas. Spray developing
5	17–21	fresh breeze	Moderate, long waves; many white horses		
6	22–27	strong breeze	Large waves, white crests extensive. Some spray	4–6 rolls in main; storm jib. Leeway affects windward course. Waves begin to stop her	Throttle back; heavy rollin in beam sea
7	28–33	near gale	Sea heaps; white foam with breakers blown in streaks. Spray seen	Residual windward progress equalled by sagging to leeward.	Should have been in shelter. Make slowly windward/leeward never
8	34–40	gale	Higher, longer waves; crests break as spray. Foam streaks large	Heavily reefed main & smallest jib. Running risky. Crew stamina matters	more than 45° from sea-course. Engine stopping risk. Cross seas dangerous in confused tidal waters.
9	41–47	strong gale	High waves, crests tumble. Dense foam streaks. Spray affects visibility	Survival only. Tow warps. Windward work impossible. Lie head up, with smallest sail or a'hull. Drift to leeward 2–3 knots	Survival only. May tow drogues or lie-to with engine slow ahead. Avoid exposed haven entrance where seas confused. Fuel shortage new danger
10	48–55	storm	Very high waves with heavy tumbling over-hanging crests. Foam in large patches & streaks. Visibility reduced		
11	56–63	violent storm	Exceptional waves (hiding small ships in hollows). All crests blown; foam covers surface. Visibility reduced.		
12	64 +	hurricane	Air filled with foam & spray. Mountainous seas completely white. Visibility very reduced.		

Harbour Buoys, Lights and Signals

In 1979 the International Association of Lighthouse Authorities (IALA) established a buoyage system for worldwide use which is easier to see and will eventually replace all local systems and signs (p.120–1).

The top of each Cardinal Mark (**CM**) indicates its compass bearing – N, S, E or W – from the point of danger. All have quick flashing lights: a long flash after the quicks identifies a south mark.

SWM Safe Water Mark: midchannel or landfall. One long white flash every 10 secs.

IDM Isolated Danger Mark: navigable water all round; flashes groups of 2.

PHB/SHB Port/Starboard Hand Buoys on entry. Lights any rhythm.

SM/TM Special Mark draws attention to e.g. Transit Marks whose alignment gives the run of e.g. a cable or sewer.

LL Leading Lights.

Lights. Each buoy shows a light with characteristics different from all others in the neighbourhood. The colour and rhythm is marked on the chart, with numbers in a group and time intervals in seconds, using this code:

Alt.   alternates in colour in successive flashes
F.   fixed continuous light
Fl.   single flash at regular intervals
F.Fl.   fixed, with one brilliant flash at regular intervals
F.Gp.Fl.   fixed, with two or more flashes at regular intervals
Gp.Fl.   two or more flashes at regular intervals
Occ.   occulting: steady light with total eclipse at regular intervals
Gp.Occ.   two or more eclipses at regular intervals
Qk.Fl.   quick flashing at 50–60 per minute
Iso.   isophase: duration of light and dark equal
L.Fl.   long flashing: flash of 2 or more seconds

Manoeuvring Hoots

1 short blast   — altering course to starboard
2 short blasts   — altering course to port
3 short blasts   — going astern
2 long + 1 short   — overtaking on your starboard side
2 long + 2 short   — overtaking on your port side
long-short-long-short — agree your signal

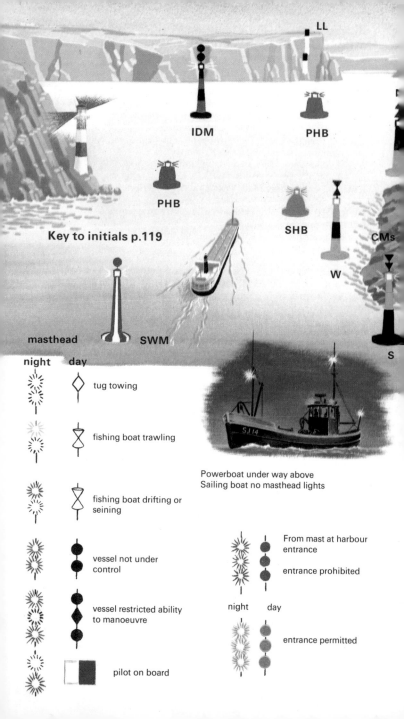

LL

IDM

PHB

PHB

SHB

CMs

W

Key to initials p.119

SWM

masthead

S

night   day

tug towing

fishing boat trawling

fishing boat drifting or
seining

vessel not under
control

vessel restricted ability
to manoeuvre

pilot on board

Powerboat under way above
Sailing boat no masthead lights

From mast at harbour
entrance

entrance prohibited

night   day

entrance permitted

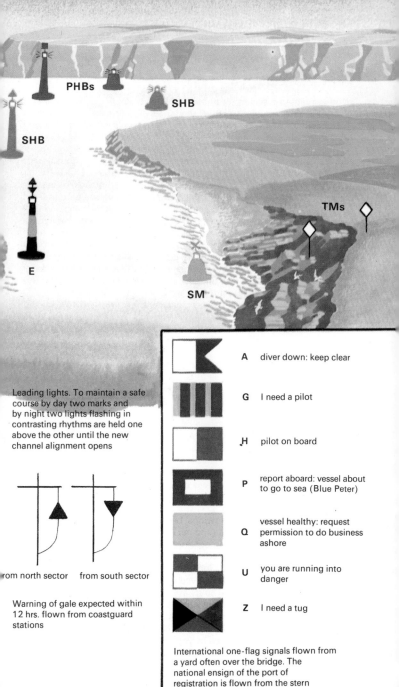

PHBs

SHB

SHB

E

TMs

SM

Leading lights. To maintain a safe course by day two marks and by night two lights flashing in contrasting rhythms are held one above the other until the new channel alignment opens

from north sector   from south sector

Warning of gale expected within 12 hrs. flown from coastguard stations

	A	diver down: keep clear
	G	I need a pilot
	H	pilot on board
	P	report aboard: vessel about to go to sea (Blue Peter)
	Q	vessel healthy: request permission to do business ashore
	U	you are running into danger
	Z	I need a tug

International one-flag signals flown from a yard often over the bridge. The national ensign of the port of registration is flown from the stern

Things to do

Nothing replaces seeing for oneself, touching, smelling and listening to living animals and plants with all the forces of nature acting upon them. Never mind science for a moment, let the beauty sink in – the colours, movements and adaptations to a hard life are all worth knowing for their own sakes. Then, a little later when the questions start to flow, turn to books for the answers. However, recognise at once the insidious illusion that understanding can spring from just reading books and watching television. Nothing, but nothing, replaces going out in all weathers and seasons to look again more closely at what has been seen before. By all means take books out with you, refer from the field to the page and back again. The books will mightily enlighten the seeing; they can never replace it.

Only renowned specialists find it useful to study the natural history of an unknown organism. The rest of us ask almost at once for the identity of the common plants and animals before us. Finding out is not the daunting task it so often appears. Use the relevant books carefully; pay the author the compliment of finding out how his book works. Be content in early days with slow progress, and accept that identification down to species or genus or even family (p.4) may be too technical. However, a sandhopper is a sandhopper is an Amphipod – we have him now in the right Order. That is progress. A sea-mat is a Polyzoan. Now we have key-words that index the natural history.

That being said, many plants and animals can be specifically identified by anybody taking the trouble to be careful, with access to the relevant books (p.124). The only indispensable tool is a handlens with magnification ×6 to ×10. *Never* be without it.

So, wherever one may be, first look, enjoy and look again. Then learn to identify within sensible limits the commonest plants and animals of the habitat. Have a hardback notebook (nobody can write in a floppy one). Make a list of plants and animals down the left margin: head vertical columns with the name of the beach, marsh, cliff and so on, the date of visit, state of tide, weather; then record each species as it occurs using the initial letter of one of the degrees of abundance – Abundant, Frequent, Common, Occasional, Rare. Already the makings of a distribution study begin to appear.

Supplement notes with drawings; better still, paintings. No matter how awful your drawings may be (and mine are worse), they are always more useful than photogaphs. Of course photographs supplement drawings; but a beginner is so concerned with all those nobs and numbers that he seldom sees what the camera looks at.

On the shore big stones are moved to see what is under them: on land, fallen logs are rolled over. 'Things live under stones because conditions suit them there; others are more suited to life in the open. Turn the stone over and leave it so, and both populations are exterminated. This is a grievous and all too common mistake. Never let it be said that there was any mark in the habitat caused by your passing.

Experiments

At low tide mark several limpet shells, each with its own combination of spots of paint or nail varnish; mark the rock just above with the same code. Knock off the limpets and put them a measured distance (recorded in your notebook) from their 'homes' (p.53). Return when the tide next uncovers them. From how far can they return to their original 'home'? Can they move equally far up, down, sideways, up and over an intervening peak?

From a very sheltered shore collect twenty living dogwhelks. Measure the total length of each shell and the maximum length of their mouth. Calculate a ratio of average mouth to average total length. Repeat on a very exposed shore and then on intermediate shores. Plot the ratios. Do they confirm what is said on p.52?

Some say that, at low tide, dark green flat winkles (p.37) are in no danger on top of the wracks because their shape and colour disguises them as bladders, while the bright yellow ones escape passing oyster-catchers by sheltering under the wracks. Mark out a 3 m square on wracks at about LWNT and test the validity of the statement.

Explore with a torch the splash zone at night. Where do all the bristle-tails and sea-slaters (p.42) go by day?

Go gently schnorkling at high tide over a length of sheltered rocky shore you have looked at on foot at low tide. It is hard to believe it is the same shore. What are the biggest differences?

From August to March most waders feed in flocks on mudflats, etc. Where do they go at high tide?

Collecting shells. Shells are not attacked by pests; they do not rot or smell. The collector has only to wash them in soapy water and dry thoroughly. Tiny ones are best cleaned in spirit. Since varnish discolours and cracks, shell surfaces are best burnished with a few drops of fine oil, rubbed over gently from time to time. Colours fade fast in alcohol and formalin destroys a shell.

Trays that fit into a larger drawer can easily be subdivided. Gum each specimen to a card on which is written, in Indian ink, its name, date and place of finding, with some indication of abundance. A good collection would include the size and colour ranges of each species and, in bivalves, growth rings showing their age range. Damaged specimens are useful until better ones replace them.

Confine collecting to empty shells. No collector has the right to kill an animal just to acquire its shell. By all means swap, but remember that there is no skill whatever in buying.

Practical help comes from joining your County Naturalists Trust (address from The Royal Society for Nature Conservation, The Green, Nettleham, Lincoln LN2 2NR) or the Royal Society for the Protection of Birds (The Lodge, Sandy, Beds SG19 2DL). The business of most bird observatories is coastal natural history, not just birds; details from the British Trust for Ornithology, Beech Grove, Tring, Herts HP23 5NR.

Courses of instruction in all kinds of coastal natural history are run by the Field Studies Council, Preston Montford, Shrewsbury SY4 1HW.

Books for Reading & Reference

These books show the way accurately and intelligibly to the beginner who is ready to take a little trouble to understand new ideas. Most of them include more detailed bibliographies.

Widely descriptive of different aspects of the coast

Barrett, John (1974): *Life on the Sea Shore*. Collins
Cramp, S., Bourne, W. R. P. & Saunders, David (1974): *The Seabirds of Britain & Ireland*. Collins
Hardy, Alister (1956): *The Open Sea: The World of Plankton*. Collins
Hardy, Alister (1959): *The Open Sea: Fish & Fisheries*. Collins
Hepburn, Ian (1952): *Flowers of the Coast*. Collins
Russell, F. S. & Yonge, C. M. (3rd. ed. 1963): *The Seas*. Warne
Steers, J. A. (1953): *The Sea Coast*. Collins (geology, scenery)
Yonge, C. M. (1949): *The Sea Shore*. Collins

Also note

On the Seashore, Animals with Shells and *Fishes*, all ed. 1969 in Macdonald Junior Reference Library; and booklets by Heather Angel with splendid coloured photographs, published by Jarrold, *Seashore Life on Sandy Beaches* (1975), *On Rocky Shores* (1975), *Sea Shells on the Seashore Bks. 1 & 2* (1978), *Seaweeds on the Seashore* (1977), *Life in our Estuaries* (1977).

A first rate, simple, illustrated introduction to the biology of the invertebrates is

Buchsbaum, Ralph (1953): *Animals without Backbones*. 2 vols. Penguin.

For Identification

Barnes, Richard (1979): *Coasts & Estuaries*. Hodder & Stoughton
Barrett, John & Yonge, C. M. (1972): *Collins Pocket Guide to the Sea Shore*. Collins
Brightman, F. H. & Nicholson, B. E. (1966): *The Oxford Book of Flowerless Plants*. Oxford. Good for seaweeds.
Campbell, A. C. (1976): *Hamlyn Guide to the Seashore and Shallow Seas of Britain and Europe*. Hamlyn
Dickinson, Carola (1963): *British Seaweeds*. Eyre & Spottiswoode
Fitter, R. & A. and Blamey, Marjorie (1974): *The Wild Flowers of Britain & Northern Europe*. Collins.
Graham, Alistair (1971): *British Prosobranchs* (i.e. snails) Synopses of Brit. Fauna, no. 2, Linnean Soc. & Academic Press
Hiscock, S. (1979). *A Field Key to the British Brown Seaweeds*. Field Studies Council, Juniper Hall, Dorking, Surrey RH5 6DA

McClintock, David & Fitter, R. S. R. (1956): *Collins Pocket Guide to Wild Flowers*. Collins

McMillan, Nora F. (1968): *British Shells*. Warne

Muus, Bent J. (1974): *Collins Guide to the Sea Fishes of Britain & North-Western Europe*. Collins

Nichols, David, Cooke, John, & Whitely, Derek (1971): *The Oxford Book of Invertebrates*. Oxford

Peterson, R. Mountfort, G. & Hollom, P. A. D. (1974): *A Field Guide to the Birds of Britain & Europe*. Collins

Tebble, Norman (1966): *British Bivalve Seashells*. Brit. Mus. Nat. Hist.

Wheeler, Alwyne (1969): *The Fishes of the British Isles & Northwest Europe*. Macmillan

In addition to all those listed I must acknowledge the help I have had from so many whose works are also on my shelves, notably

Bellamy, David (1975): *The Life-giving Sea*. Hamish Hamilton

Flemming, N. C. ed. (1977): *The Undersea*. Cassell

Green, J. (1968): *The Biology of Estuarine Animals*. Sidgwick & Jackson

Lewis, J. R. (1964): *The Ecology of Rocky Shores*. EUP

Moore, Hilary B. (1958): *Marine Ecology*. John Wiley

Newell, R. C. (1970): *Biology of Intertidal Animals*. Logos

Southward, A. J. (1965): *Life on the Seashore*. Heinemann

Stephenson, T. A. & Anne (1972): *Life between Tidemarks on Rocky Shores*. Freeman

With profound thanks to so many, the mistakes in this book are still all my own.

John H. Barrett

Index

This complements the larger references in the Pictorial Key, pp.4–9. The alphabetical series gives priority to widely accepted vernacular names. Where one does not exist, the scientific name is perforce cited alone. In some cases the scientific has been added to a doubtful vernacular.

Lesser textual references are in normal type; primary text and illustrations in bold; lesser illustrations in italics.

Alder 104
Amphipoda ('sandhoppers') 73, 86, **87**, 99, **108**, 110: *Chelura terebrans* **117**; *Corophium* sp. 106, **109**, 110; *Gammarus* sp. **59**
Auger (Tower) -shell **87**
Auk, Little **26**

Barnacles, Acorn 15, **36**, **38**, **40**, 47, 52, 53, 71, 73: *Balanus balanoides* **36**, 47; *B. crenatus* **36**; *B. improvisus* **108**; *Chthamalus stellatus* **36**, 47; *Elminius modestus* **36**, parasitic: *Sacculina carcini* **60**, *61*
Bass **84**
Beans, West Indian: *Entada gigas* **90**, *Mucuna urens* **90**
Belemnites **86**
Blennies **36**: Butterfly **70**; Common **70**, **71**; Tompot **66**
Bittersweet **96**
Bonnet-shell **87**
Bootlace-weed **67**, **84**
Bootlace-worm **82**
Brittle-stars: *Acronida brachiata* **81**; *Ophiura* sp. **84**
Bugloss, Viper's **93**

Carpet-shell **77**
Carrot, Wild *24*
Cat-worms **83**
Chlorophyll 14, 56
Chough **26**
Clams, see Scallops
Coat-of-Mail Shell (Chiton): *Acanthochitona crinitus* **53**; *Lepidochitona cinereus* **53**
Cod 15, 78, 107, **115**
Cockle **80**, 110: Common **81**; Dog **76**; Prickly **81**
Comb-jellies **51**
Corals 51, 54: Devonshire Cup **51**; Soft *Alcyonium digitatum* **90**, **116**
Coral-weed 47, **54**
Cord-grass (*Spartina*) **100**, **101**
Corkwing **116**
Cormorant **114**
Cowries **65**

Crabs 15, 20, **60**, 84, 85, 110: Edible **61**; Hairy **60**; Hermit, Common **84**, *Eupagurus prideauxi* 84; Masked **79**; Porcelain, Broad-clawed **60**, Long-clawed **60**; Shore **61**, *68*; Spider, *Macropodia rostrata* **85**, *Maia squinado* **66**; Swimming, Velvet **61**; *Xantho incisus* **60**
Crawfish (Spiny Lobster) **69**
Crow, Carrion **26**; Hooded **26**
Curlew *39*, **94**, 110
Cuttlefish 20, 39, 85, 86: Common **86**, **112**; Little **112**

Dab **106**
Dabchick (Little Grebe) 110, **111**
Dead-men's Fingers **90**, **116**
Desiccation 28, 32, 42, 45, 117
Diver, Great Northern **23**; Red-throated **23**
Dock, Curled **96**
Dogfish, egg-case **85**, **86**: Lesser-spotted **115**
Dogwhelk, Common 36, 47, **52**, **53**, 73; Netted **65**
Dolphin: Bottle-nosed **20**; Common **20**; White-sided **20**
Dosinia lupinus **77**
Dove, Rock **26**
Dunlin **94**, 110
Dulse **47**

Eel, Common **107**; Conger **115**; Sand 18, 26, **78**, 85, 115
Eelgrass (*Zostera*) 23, 98, 110, **112**, **113**
Eelpout **116**
Eider-duck **22**
Energy 14, 17, 76

Fan-worms **82**
Father-lasher **71**
Feather-star **117**
Filograna implexa **62**
Fish 15, 17, 20, 39, **71**, **106**,

110, **112**, **115**, **116**
Flask-shell **63**
Flat-worm **108**
Flounder **106**
Food Chains 14, 17, 18, **115**
Fulmar **25**
Furrow-shell **109**

Gannet *18*
Gaper-shell, Blunt **79**; Sand **79**
Gibbula magus **37**
Glasswort **98**, 99, **100**, 101, 110
Goby, Black **116**; Common **106**; Rock **71**
Godwit, Bar-tailed **94**, **110**; Black-tailed **110**
Goldeneye 110, **111**
Goose, Barnacle **23**, 88; Brent **23**, 112
Greenshank 110, **111**
Gribble **117**
Guillemot, Black **26**; Bridled & Common **26**
Gulls, Black-backed, Great **22**, **25**, *114*, Lesser **25**; Black-headed **114**; Common **25**; Glaucous **22**; Herring **25**, *114*

Haddock **107**
Halophytes 45, 98
Heart-shell **87**
Herb-Robert **96**
Heron *97*, *100*, *110*, **111**
Herring 107, 115
Hiatella sp. **63**
Hydrobia ulvae & *H. ventrosa* 99, **108**, 110
Hydroides norvegica **62**
Hydroids (Sea-Firs) **51**, 73, 85: *Dynamena pumila* **55**; *Hydractinia echinata* **86**; *Kirchenpaueria pinnata* **117**; *Laomedea flexuosa* **117**; *Obelia geniculata* **55**; *Plumularia pinnata* **117**; *Tubularia larynx* **117**

Idotea spp. 110, **113**
Insects 106: Bristle-tail *Petrobius maritimus* **42**;

Spring-tail *Lipura*
(=*Anurida*) *maritima* **55**
Interstitial Space 74

Jackdaw **26**
Jellyfish 15, 20, 51: *Aurelia*
aurita **18**; By-the-Wind-
Sailor **18**; *Chrysaora*
isosceles **19**; *Cyanea lamarki*
18; *Pelagia noctiluca* **18**;
Portuguese Man-o'-War **18**;
Rhizostoma pulmo **18**;
Stalked- *Haliclystus auricula*
113

Kittiwake *18*, **25**
Knot **110**

Lamprey, Sea **107**
Lanice conchilega **82**
Lichens 38, *41*, **43**, 92, *95*:
Caloplaca marina **43**;
Lecanora atra **43**; *Lichina*
confinis **43**; *Ochrolechia*
parella **43**; *Ramalina* sp. **43**;
Verrucaria maura **43**;
Xanthoria parietina **43**
Light **13**, *32*, **49**, 54, 56, 73
Limpet 35, 38, 47, *52*, **53**, *58*:
Blue-rayed **66**, **67**; Bonnet
87; Chinaman's-hat **65**;
Common **52**, *55*, *58*, 73, **87**;
Keyhole **65**; Slipper **76**; Slit
65; Tortoiseshell **65**
Lineus ruber **59**
Lobster, Common **69**; Squat
68, 69
Long-tailed Duck **22**
Lug-worm **82**, 110
Lumpsucker **85**

Mackerel 18, 78, 107, **115**
Mallard 110, **111**
Mallow, Tree *26*
Marram-grass **88**, **92**
Mermaid's Purse **85**, **86**
Mud, structure 13, 74, **98**,
100, 104, 109
Mullet, Grey **106**
Mussels 16, **38**, *47*, 68, 110:
Bearded **67**; Edible **40**, **47**;
Horse **67**
Mysids **51**, 107, **113**

Necklace-shell **78**
Needle-shell **87**

Oarweeds (Tangles, Kelps) *38*,
40, 47, 49, **64**, **66**, 88
Orache, Common **95**
Osmosis 106
Otter *22*
Otter-shell **80**
Oyster, Native *63*, **76**;
Portuguese **76**; Saddle **53**

Oystercatcher **40**, *64*, 110

Paddle-worms **53**, **65**, **83**
Peacock-worms **82**
Peewit (Lapwing) **110**
Pelican's-foot **87**
Peregrine Falcon **22**
Periwinkle, see Winkle
pH **12**, 55, 92
Pharus legumen **80**, **81**
Photosynthesis 12, **14**, 32, 43,
55, 56
Piddock, Common **63**; Oval **63**
Pike **107**
Pilchard 115
Pipefish, Greater **112**; Worm
112
Pipit, Rock **41**, 42
Plaice 15, **106**
Plankton **14**–**17**, 18, 20, 25,
29, 35, 36, 42, 53, 58, 60,
62, 64, 67, 71, 78, **115**
Plantain, Buck's-horn **45**; Sea
45, **102**
Plover, Golden **110**; Grey **94**,
110; Ringed *38*, **73**, **96**
Pollack 26, **115**
Polydora sp. **63**
Pomatoceros triqueter 58, **62**
Poppy, Yellow-horned **96**
Porpoise 18, **20**
Potamopyrgus jenkinsi, **108**
Prawn 78, 85: Aesop **50**;
Common **50**; Freshwater
108
Procerodes sp. **108**
Protula tubularia **62**
Puffin **25**

Rabbit 88, *93*, 95
Rag-worms **82**, 83, 106, **109**,
110
Ragwort 92
Raven **26**
Ray, Thornback 85, **115**
Razorbill **26**
Razor-shells **80**, **81**
Red Fescue Grass **41**, **45**
Redshank **73**, 110, **111**
Red-thread Worm **59**
Reeds/Rushes **104**; Reed,
Common 104, **105**; Rush,
Saltmarsh *Juncus gerardi*
105; Sea- *J. maritimus* 99,
105; Sea-club *Scirpus*
maritimus 104, **105**
Rissoa parva **87**
Rockling, Three-bearded **70**

Salinity **12**, 32, **45**, 55, 75, **99**,
106, **108**, **113**
Salmon 107
Saltwort *Salsola kali* **91**
Samphire, Golden **45**; Marsh
100; Rock **27**, **45**

Sand Couch-grass **91**, 92
Sanderling **91**, **94**
Sandhoppers, see Amphipoda
Sandpiper, Curlew **110**, 111;
Purple *40*
Sand-tube Worm (*Sabellaria*)
62
Scale-worms **59**, **82**, **83**
Scallop 68: Great **77**; Queen
90; Variegated **77**
Scoter, Common **22**; Velvet **22**
Scurvy-grass, Common **45**;
Long-leaved **103**

Sea-anemones **51**: Beadlet 47,
56; Burrowing *Peachia*
hastata **80**, **81**; *Cereus*
pedunculatus **81**; Dahlia **51**;
Gem (Wartlet) **56**; on
hermit-crabs *Adamsia*
palliata & *Calliactis*
parasitica **84**; Plumose **116**;
Sagartia elegans **51**;
Snakelocks **56**
Sea-arrowgrass **102**
Sea-aster **103**, **104**
Sea-beet 91, **95**
Sea-bindweed **92**
Sea-blight, Annual (*Suaeda*
maritima) **100**, **101**;
Shrubby (*S. fruticosa*) **96**,
104
Sea-buckthorn **93**
Sea-campion *24*, **94**, **95**
Sea Club-rush **104**, **105**
Sea-cucumber **112**
Sea-firs, see Hydroids
Sea-gooseberries *Beroë*
cucumiformis &
Pleurobrachia pileus **51**
Sea-hare **67**
Sea-heath (*Franconia laevis*)
104
Sea-holly **93**
Sea-lavender, Common 99,
100, **102**, **103**; Rock **45**
Sea-lemon **56**
Sea-lettuce **54**
Sea-mats (Polyzoa) **64**: *Flustra*
foliacea **90**; *Flustrella*
hispida **47**; *Membranipora*
membranacea **64**
Sea-mayweed **95**
Sea Meadow-grass 99, **102**,
103
Sea-milkwort **104**
Sea-mouse **82**, 83
Sea-pea **96**
Sea-pink *24*, *41*, **45**, 99, 102,
103
Sea-potato 80, **81**
Sea-purslane **99**, **101**
Sea-radish **91**

Sea-rocket **91**
Sea-rush 99, **105**
Sea-sandwort 91, **95**
Sea-slater **42**, 73
Sea-slugs: *Actaeon tornatilis*
78; *Aeolidia papillosa* 51,
56; *Akera bullata* **113**;
Alderia modesta **113**; Sea-
Hare *Aplysia modesta* **67**;
Sea-Lemon *Archidoris
pseudoargus* **56**
Sea-snail, Montagu's **71**
Sea-spleenwort **45**
Sea-spurrey, Greater **102**;
Lesser **102**; Rock **45**
Sea-squirts (Tunicata):
Ascidiella aspersa **116**;
Ciona intestinalis **116**;
Clavellina lepadiformis **116**;
Star Ascidian *Botryllus
schlosseri* **58**, **116**
Sea-trout **106**
Sea-urchins: Common **116**;
Heart **80**, **81**; *Paracentrotus
lividus* **63**; *Psammechinus
miliaris* **65**; test (shell) **81**
Seaweeds 12, 32, **34**, 38, **46**,
48, **50**, 53, 55, **84**, **85**, 98;
colours **56**; holdfasts **57**, 66;
reproduction 56
Browns: *Alaria esculenta* **47**,
48, **67**; *Bifurcaria rotunda*
56; Bootlace *Chorda filum*
67, **84**; *Desmarestia
ligulata* **70**; *Dictyota
dichotoma* **55**; *Halidrys
siliquosa* **85**; Oarweeds
Laminaria spp. **38**, **40**, 47,
49, *64*, **66**; *L. saccharina*
84; *Saccorhiza
polyschides* **67**; *Padina
pavonina* **55**; *Scytosiphon
lomentaria* **55**;
Thongweed *Himanthalia
elongata* **47**; Wracks 23,
35, 36, 52, 73: Bladder
Fucus vesiculosus **35**, **40**;
Channel *Pelvetia
canaliculata* **35**, **40**, 73;
Egg (Knotted)
Ascophyllum nodosum
34, **40**, *55*, 72, *73*;
F. ceranoides **35**; Flat
(Spiral) *F. spiralis* **35**, **40**,
73; Saw *F. serratus* **35**,
40;
Greens: *Bryopsis plumosa*
57; *Cladophora rupestris*
53; *Codium tomentosum*
57; *Enteromorpha* sp. **52**;
E. linza **57**; Sea-lettuce
Ulva lactuca **54**;
Reds: *Apoglossum
ruscifolium* **48**; *Bostrichia
scorpioides* **99**, **101**;

Callblepharis sp. **50**;
Callophyllis laciniata **50**;
Ceramium rubrum **48**;
Chondrus crispus **57**;
Coral Weed *Corallina
officinalis* 47, **54**;
Delesseria sanguinea **50**;
Dilsea carnosa **85**; Dulse
Gigartina stellata **47**;
Gastroclonium ovatum **48**;
Gracilaria verrucosa **85**;
Griffithsia flosculosa **56**;
Heterosiphonia plumosa
50; *Hypoglossum
woodwardii* **48**; *Laurencia
pinnatifida* **53**;
Lithophyllum spp. **54**;
Lithothamnion spp. 47, **54**;
Lomentaria articulata **48**;
Membranoptera alata **48**;
Phycodrys rubens **50**;
Plocamium coccineum **48**;
Plumaria elegans **48**;
Polysiphonia fastigiata **34**;
Rhodymenia palmata **66**
Sedge, Sand **92**
Shag **26**
Serpula vermicularis **62**
Shark, Basking **20**; Blue **20**
Shearwater, Manx *20*
Shelduck **110**
Shells (Mollusca) **88**:
collecting **123**; structure 37,
76
Shipworm **63**, **117**
Shrimps 85, 99, 106, 110:
Burrowing **112**; Common
108; Freshwater *108*; Ghost
55; Opossum 51, 106, **113**
Skate 86, **115**
Skua, Arctic *18*
Snipe *104*
Sorrel *24*
Sphaeroma sp. 99, **108**
Spirorbis spp. **35**, **62**
Sponges **58**: 'bath' **86**; Boring
63; Breadcrumb **58**;
Hymeniacidon sanguinea
58; *Myxilla* sp. **58**, **84**; Purse
48; *Suberites domuncula* **85**
Sprat 26, **106**, 115
Spurge, Portland **93**; Sea- **93**
Squid, see Cuttlefish
Star-ascidian **58**, **116**
Starfish **68**: *Astropecten
irregularis* **78**, **79**; Common
69; Cushion-star **58**;
Henricia occulata **66**;
Marthasterias glacialis **67**;
Palmipes membranaceus
68; *Porania pulvillus* **68**;
Sunstar, Common **69**,
Purple **67**
Stickleback, Fifteen-spined
107; Three-spined **107**

Stonechat **97**
Stonecrop, Biting **96**; English
45
Stonemason-worm **82**
Sucker, Cornish **70**;
Two-spotted **70**
Sunfish **20**
Sunset-shell **78**
Symbiosis 43, **85**

Teal **110**
Tellin, Baltic **109**, 110; Thin **78**
Tern, Arctic **90**; Common **91**;
Little **91**; Roseate **90**;
Sandwich **91**
Thongweed **47**
Thrift (Sea-Pink) **41**, **45**, 99,
· 102, 103
Tope **20**
Top-shells 35, 37: Common
37; Grey **37**; Grooved **113**;
Painted **37**; Purple **37**
Trough-shell, Rayed **77**; Thick
77
Tubulanus annulatus **82**
Turbidity **13**, 32, 109
Turnstone **40**, **94**
Turtle, Loggerhead **20**
Tusk-shell **87**

Venus-shells **79**
Violet Snail **87**

Water-rail *104*
Weaver, Lesser **78**
Wedge-shell 74, **78**
Wentletrap **87**
Whale, Blue **17**; Killer **20**
Wheatear **97**
Whelk, Common **76**, eggs **86**
Whimbrel **94**
Whitebait, see Sprat & Herring
fry
Whiting **115**
Wigeon 23, *101*, 110, **111**
Winkle 35, **37**, 40: Edible **37**;
Flat **37**, 73; Rough **37**, **42**,
73; Small **37**, **42**, 47; Sting
65
Worms 15, **35**, **53**, **59**, **62**, **63**,
65, 71, 75, **82**, **83**, 85, 106,
108, **109**, 110
Wracks 23, 35, 36, 52, **73**,
88: Bladder **35**, *37*, **40**;
Channel **35**, **40**, 73; Egg
(Knotted) **34**, **40**, *55*, 72,
73; Flat (Spiral) **35**, **40**, *72*,
73, Saw **35**, **40**
Wrasse, Corkwing **116**;
Cuckoo **66**

Yellow-wort **93**

Zonation 30, 32, 43, 45, 47,
56, **72**

Have fun with
Arts and Crafts
Pirates

Rita Storey

W

FRANKLIN WATTS
LONDON • SYDNEY

First published in 2012 by
Franklin Watts
338 Euston Road
London NW1 3BH

Franklin Watts Australia
Level 17/207 Kent Street
Sydney NSW 2000

Series editor: Amy Stephenson

Packaged for Franklin Watts by Storeybooks
rita@storeybooks.co.uk
Designer: Rita Storey
Editor: Nicola Barber
Crafts: Rita Storey
Photography: Tudor Photography, Banbury
www.tudorphotography.co.uk

A CIP catalogue record for this book is available
from the British Library.

Printed in China

Dewey classification: 745.5

ISBN 978 1 4451 1068 4

Cover images Shutterstock (top left), Tudor Photography, Banbury

Franklin Watts is a division of Hachette Children's Books,
an Hachette UK company
www.hachette.co.uk

Before you start

Some of the projects in this book require scissors, paint, glue,
a sewing needle or an oven. When using these things we
would recommend that children are supervised by
a responsible adult.

Contents

Captain Jack's Pirate Hat 4

'Eye-spy' Spyglass 6

Pirate Outfit 8

Hardtack Biscuits 10

Pirate Treasure Chest 12

Treasure Map Game 14

Deep-sea Octopus 16

A Motley Crew 18

A Ghostly Pirate Ship 20

The Captain's Parrot 22

Into the Deep 24

Shipwreck in the Ocean 26

A Pirate Compass 28

Templates 30

Further Information and Index 32

Captain Jack's Pirate Hat

Ahoy there! Come aboard our pirate ship and make a tricorne (three-cornered hat) to wear. This hat is just like the one worn by Captain Jack Sparrow in 'Pirates of the Caribbean'.

To make a swashbuckling captain's hat you will need

- strong brown paper 50cm square
- pencil
- string about 30cm long
- masking tape
- scissors
- strong brown paper 40cm square
- mixing bowl 20cm across
- glue
- dark brown paint and large paintbrush
- 3 pins
- needle and embroidery thread

1 Screw the large piece of brown paper into a ball. Flatten it out again. Fold it in half and then into quarters.

2 Tie the pencil to the string so that the string is the length of one side of the paper. Tape the other end of the string to the corner of the paper where all the folds meet.

3 Holding the string tight, draw a quarter circle on the paper from corner to corner.

4 Shorten the string to 9cm long and draw a second quarter circle. Carefully remove the tape. Cut out along the pencil lines. Open out the paper. This will be the brim of the hat.

5 Repeat stages 1 – 3 with the smaller piece of brown paper. Cut out along the pencil lines.

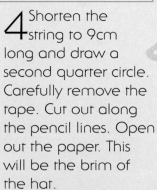

6 Turn the bowl upside down. To make the crown of the hat, squash the smaller circle of paper over the upturned bowl. Put strips of masking tape around the crown 2cm from the bottom edge of the bowl. Remove the paper hat from the bowl. Trim off the edges.

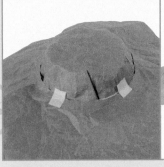

7 Drop the brim of the hat over the crown. Use four small pieces of masking tape to lightly tape the brim to the crown.

8 Turn the hat over and rest the crown in the bowl. Make small cuts in the tape, about 2cm apart, down to where it meets the brim.

9 Take the hat out of the bowl and turn it over. Carefully peel off the four pieces of masking tape and remove the brim. Bend the flaps out. Spread glue on to the flaps.

10 Drop the brim down over the crown and press it on to the flaps. Leave to dry.

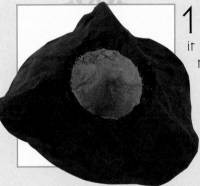

11 Paint the hat and leave it to dry. Then turn the hat over and paint the underside of the brim. Leave to dry.

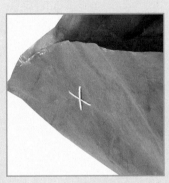

12 To create a tricorne shape, fold the brim of the hat up to the crown in three places, equally spaced around the crown. Pin the edges of the brim together where they come to a point. Thread the needle with a length of embroidery thread and tie a knot in the end. Push the needle through the brim where it is pinned. Make two stitches at right angles to each other to make a cross. Knot the end of the thread at the back. Repeat by the other two pins. Remove the pins.

Aye, aye, Captain!

'Eye-spy' Spyglass

Pirates were always on the lookout for ships to plunder. You too can scan the horizon with this spyglass. It's easy to make and moves just like the real thing.

To make a super spyglass you will need

- two tubes, one slightly thinner than the other
- scissors
- clingwrap and an elastic band
- wrapping paper
- sticky tape
- coloured card
- PVA glue

1 Make small cuts about 5mm long and 5mm apart in the end of the larger cardboard tube to make flaps.

2 Bend the flaps in towards the inside of the tube.

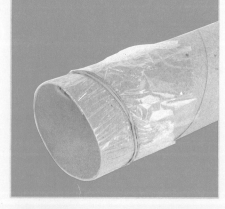

3 Tightly stretch a piece of clingwrap across the other end. Secure with an elastic band.

4 Cut a piece of wrapping paper to cover each tube. Each piece should be the same length as a tube and wide enough to wrap round it.

5 Secure the paper with sticky tape.

6 Push the small tube into the end of the large one. The small tube should slide in and out of the large one just like a real spyglass. The flaps will hold the small tube in place.

7 Cut strips of coloured card long enough to wrap round the tubes. Glue them in place around the ends of the tubes.

Put the end of the small tube up to your eye and keep a watch for enemy ships on the horizon.

Ship ahoy on the starboard side, Captain!

Spyglass

A spyglass is a type of small telescope that can be collapsed and carried around in a pocket. Pirates used spyglasses to scan the distant horizon for ships.

Pirate Outfit

Cutlass

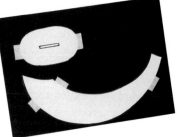

A pirate lad or lass only had one set of clothes – the ones they were wearing. Pressgang your old clothes and add these pirate accessories to make a swashbuckling pirate outfit.

1 Copy the template for the cutlass blade and hand guard on page 30 – 31 on to the card.

2 Tape the shapes on to the poster board with masking tape. Draw round the shapes. Cut them out. Cut out the slit in the handle.

To make a fearsome cutlass and a silver buckle you will need

- felt-tip pen • sheet of thin card
- scissors • masking tape • poster board
- silver paint • paintbrush

3 Paint both sides with silver paint. Leave to dry.

4 Slide the slit in the hand guard down over the blade as far as it will go.

For an eyepatch you will need

- black felt • scissors • thin ribbon

Buckle

To finish off your pirate outfit you will need

- white or striped T-shirt
- pair of black or brown trousers
- boots • long scarf
- red headscarf
- neckerchief

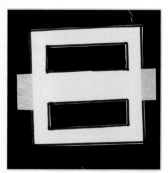

1 Follow steps 1 – 2 above but this time copy and cut out the buckle shape.

2 Paint the buckle silver. Leave to dry.

Eyepatch

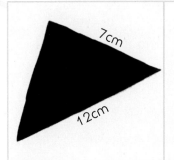

1 Cut a triangle of felt 12cm x 7cm.

2 Round off the corners. Cut a small slit in both sides of the eyepatch as shown.

3 Cut a piece of ribbon long enough to go round your head plus enough length to tie at the back. Thread the ribbon through the holes.

Pirate Outfit

1 Put on the T-shirt and trousers. Tuck the trousers into the boots. Thread the long scarf through the buckle and tie it around your waist.

2 Tie a red scarf round your head. Tie a neckerchief round your neck. Tie on your eyepatch and put on your tricorne hat (see pages 4 – 5). Brandish your cutlass – you are ready to be a real pirate!

Hardtack Biscuits

These yummy ship's biscuits are a lot nicer than the ones pirates used to eat on their long voyages. Ship's biscuits were so hard that pirates often broke their teeth on them. Pirates called them 'hardtack'.

To make pirate biscuits you will need

- 250g plain flour
- 1 teaspoon baking powder
- 125g margarine or butter
- 75g caster sugar
- 1 egg
- 1 teaspoon vanilla essence
- red and pink fondant icing
- tube of black writing icing

- bowl
- wooden spoon
- sieve
- rolling pin
- 6cm biscuit cutter
- baking tray
- wire rack

Before you start, set the oven to 180°C (350°F, gas mark 4).

1 Put the flour, baking powder, butter and caster sugar into a bowl.

2 Rub them together with your fingers (clean hands, please!) until the mixture does not have any big lumps in it.

3 Add the egg and vanilla essence.

4 Mix with the wooden spoon. Keep mixing until the mixture sticks together. Then use your hands to make the mixture into a ball of dough.

5 Sieve some flour on to a work surface.

6 Roll out the dough so that it is about 3mm thick.

7 Use the biscuit cutter to cut out 12 circles.

8 Put the biscuits on a greased baking tray. Ask a grown up to put the tray into the preheated oven. Cook for 15 minutes.

9 Ask a grown up to take the tray out of the oven. Put the cooked biscuits on a wire rack to cool. Don't forget to turn the oven off!

10 When the biscuits are cool roll out the red and pink fondant icing thinly. Cut out circles using the biscuit cutter.

11 Cut the circles in half and press a red semicircle and a pink semicircle on to each biscuit.

12 Use the black writing icing to draw on an eyepatch, an eye, a mouth and a nose. Add dots of black icing to the hat.

Make lots of biscuits as snacks for your pirate crew.

Pirate Treasure Chest

Pirates buried their treasure in strong treasure chests to hide it away from other pirates. Hide all your special loot away in this chest.

To make a treasure chest you will need

- shoe box with lid
- ruler
- pencil
- thin card
- compass
- scissors
- glue
- brown paint
- stiff brush
- gold tape or strips of gold card
- paper
- gold card
- sticky tape

1 Measure the short side of the shoe box. Draw a line the same length on the thin card. Measure half way across the line and draw a dot.

2 Put the point of the compass on the dot. Open the compass out so that the pencil is at the end of the line. Draw a semicircle. Keeping the point of the compass in the same place, open the compass out another 1cm. Draw a second semicircle outside the first.

3 Cut out the card along the line of the larger semicircle.

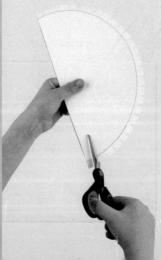

4 Cut small V-shapes from the outside of the semicircle up to the first line at 1cm intervals to make tabs. Repeat steps 1 – 3 to make another semicircle.

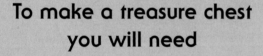

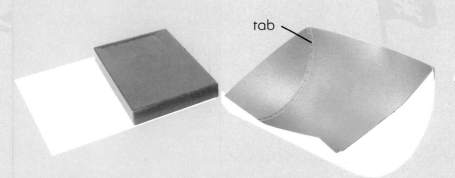

tab

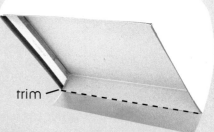

trim

5 To make the top of the treasure chest, cut a piece of card the same size as the long side of the box lid and twice the length of the short side.

6 Fold back the tabs around one of the semicircles. Glue the long piece of card to the tabs. Repeat with the second semicircle keeping the tabs on the inside of the curved shape.

7 The lid of the shoe box should fit inside the shape. Place it inside the shape and tape the straight sides of the shape on to the top of the lid of the shoe box. Trim off any card that overlaps.

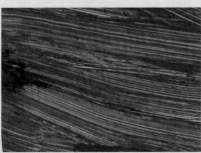

8 Paint the box with the brown paint. Use the stiff brush to make patterns in the paint to look like wood. Leave to dry. Trim the edges of the lid and base with gold tape or strips of gold card.

9 Use the templates on page 31 to trace two handles, a catch, and a lock on to paper. Cut them out. Draw round them on to gold card. Glue them on to the front and sides of the box. Fill the box with all your special treasures.

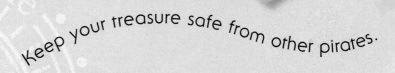

Keep your treasure safe from other pirates.

Treasure Map Game

Ahoy there mateys! Challenge your motley crew to a swashbucklin' adventure. Not for the lily-livered, this pirate voyage is full of dangers. Beware – not everyone will make it to claim the buried treasure.

To make a treasure map game you will need

- A4 sheet of card (297mm x 210mm)
- pencil, felt-tip pens, paints, crayons
- ruler
- large piece of coloured paper (317mm x 230mm)
- large piece of poster board or thick card (317mm x 230mm)
- glue
- scraps of thick card
- scissors
- a dice

1 Draw an island shape on a piece of card. Draw details such as trees, rivers and mountains on to the island.

2 Colour or paint the island and the sea round it. Divide the map into 30 squares.

3 Glue the map onto a larger piece of coloured paper. Glue the coloured paper onto poster board or thick card. Draw a treasure chest on squares 21. Number the squares from bottom left to top right starting at 1. Write 'Set sail' in square 1 and 'You win' in square 30.

4 Think of some things that could happen along the way to stop the pirates getting to their treasure. Write an instruction for what to do if you land on these squares.

5 You can use real coins as counters or you can make your own. Cut circles small enough to fit on the squares of the board from scraps of poster board or thick card. Paint or colour them to look like old Spanish coins (doubloons).

How to play the game

Each player has a counter and puts it on square 1 ('Set sail'). The first player rolls the dice. Move the counter the number of squares shown on the dice. If there is an instruction on the square do as it says. Take it in turns to throw the dice. The winner is the first one to reach the treasure and escape with it to square 30. When you get close to the square containing the treasure chest you must roll the exact number to land on it.

Aye, there be plenty of doubloons for them that get there first.

You can download the coins from www.franklinwatts.co.uk and glue them onto the circles.

Deep-sea Octopus

Pirates are always on the look-out for deadly sea monsters. This octopus, with its eight arms, is lurking ready to attack. It will eat any pirates that fall overboard as a tasty snack.

To make this crazy creature you will need

- 4 pairs of thick, clean tights
- scissors
- cushion filling
- 10 strong elastic bands
- needle and strong thread
- felt – black, white and some bright colours
- fabric glue

1 Cut the legs off the tights near to the body.

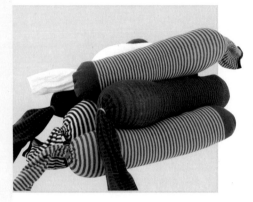

2 Stuff the legs with the cushion filling to within about 10cm of the top. Fasten the top of each one with a small elastic band.

3 Gather the top of all the legs together near the elastic bands. Use another elastic band to secure them. Twist it several times until it is tight.

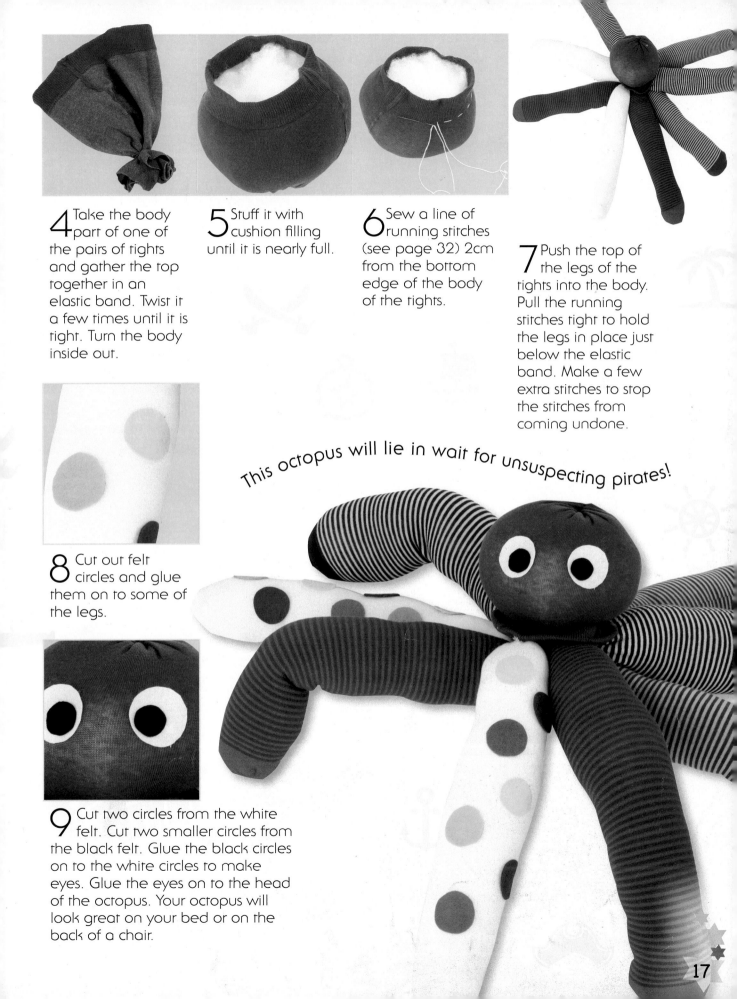

4 Take the body part of one of the pairs of tights and gather the top together in an elastic band. Twist it a few times until it is tight. Turn the body inside out.

5 Stuff it with cushion filling until it is nearly full.

6 Sew a line of running stitches (see page 32) 2cm from the bottom edge of the body of the tights.

7 Push the top of the legs of the tights into the body. Pull the running stitches tight to hold the legs in place just below the elastic band. Make a few extra stitches to stop the stitches from coming undone.

This octopus will lie in wait for unsuspecting pirates!

8 Cut out felt circles and glue them on to some of the legs.

9 Cut two circles from the white felt. Cut two smaller circles from the black felt. Glue the black circles on to the white circles to make eyes. Glue the eyes on to the head of the octopus. Your octopus will look great on your bed or on the back of a chair.

17

A Motley Crew

Pirate captains used to round up any sailors they could find to make up their crews. See what you can find lying around to create your own pirate crew of finger puppets.

To make a basic finger puppet you will need

- piece of paper • felt-tip pen
- scissors • felt • pin
- needle and thread

To make a pirate's parrot you will need

- basic finger puppet made from green felt
- glue • googly eyes
- scrap of yellow felt • scissors • feathers

To make a pirate puppet you will need

- basic finger puppet made from blue felt
- polystyrene ball
- pink paint • paintbrush
- cocktail stick • ball of plasticine
- felt-tip pen • red paint • glue
- scraps of blue, pink and brown felt
- scissors • gold and silver paper

Basic Finger Puppet

1 Draw round your finger on to the paper. Leave a 1.5cm gap all the way round. Cut out the shape.

2 Put two pieces of felt on top of each other. Pin the template to the felt. Cut out the shape.

3 Sew the two pieces together 5mm from the edge, using backstitch (see page 32). Do not stitch across the straight edge. Trim off the excess fabric.

4 Turn the shape inside out and press flat under a book.

Pirate's Parrot

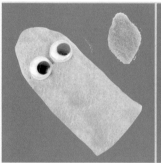

1 Glue the googly eyes on to the green finger puppet. Cut out a diamond shape for the beak. Pinch it together at one corner and glue it on to the finger puppet just below the eyes.

2 Glue feathers on to the top of the parrot at the back to make plumage. Glue feathers on to each side to make wings.

Pirate Puppet

1 Push one end of the cocktail stick into the polystyrene ball and the other end into the plasticine. Stick the plasticine on to a work surface. Paint the polystyrene ball pink. Leave to dry.

2 Use a felt-tip pen to draw on an eye, an eyebrow, a moustache and an eyepatch. Paint a red hat. Leave to dry.

3 Take the polystyrene ball off the cocktail stick. Press the top of the felt finger puppet down to make a little dent. Spread glue on the bottom of the head. Glue the head into the dent in the felt.

4 Using the template on page 31, cut out two arms from blue felt and two hands from pink felt. Glue an arm on to each side of the finger puppet's body.

7 Glue on a tiny felt beard. Cut out a cutlass (sword) from silver paper and glue it on to one hand. Use your puppets to act out a pirate story using your pirate and his parrot friend.

5 Glue a hand to the bottom of each arm.

6 To make a belt, cut a strip of brown felt long enough to go round the puppet. Glue it around the bottom of the finger puppet. Cut a square of gold paper. Colour a square in the centre. Glue it on to the belt to make a buckle.

A Ghostly Pirate Ship

There have been lots of sightings of ghost ships over the years. Make this fantastic ghost pirate ship picture to hang on your wall. The wax picture will appear through the paint like a ghostly pirate ship appearing through the sea mist.

To make this ghostly ship you will need

- A3 sheet of white paper (297mm x 420mm)
- masking tape
- blue, red and yellow wax crayons
- white candle
- watercolour paints
- big paintbrush
- piece of card 397mm x 440mm

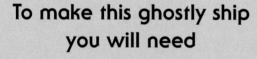

1 Tape the paper on to a work surface with the masking tape. Use the blue crayon to draw a picture of a pirate ship and lots of waves on the paper. Draw a moon with the yellow crayon. Draw portholes and flags with the red crayon.

2 Draw over the outline again with the candle. Fill in the sails and boat with the candle. Add some waves and swirling mist. Do not worry if you cannot see the candle wax – it will show on the finished picture.

3 Mix the watercolour paints with water to make runny sea colours.

4 Swish the paint across the whole paper with the big brush.

5 The paint colours the paper but will not stick to the wax, so the wax outline stays white. Leave the picture to dry.

6 Carefully peel off the masking tape. Glue the picture on to a piece of card.

The Flying Dutchman

The film 'Pirates of the Caribbean' features The Flying Dutchman, a phantom ship doomed to roam the seas. This ship is based on an old legend. According to the story, the captain of The Flying Dutchman was cursed never to sail into port, but to haunt the oceans for ever. Sailors believed that it was bad luck to catch a glimpse of this ghostly ship.

The Captain's Parrot

Pirates were often at sea for months on end. For company, they sometimes kept parrots as pets. You can make yourself a feathery friend to take on your next voyage.

To make a captain's parrot you will need

- A4 sheet of yellow paper
- A5 sheet of green paper
- A5 sheets of coloured paper
- felt-tip pen
- scissors
- pipe cleaner
- 2 googly eyes
- glue
- craft feathers
- string
- sticky tape

1 Copy the parrot template on page 30 on to a sheet of coloured paper. Cut it out.

2 Glue the small circle to the top of the oval shape.

3 Bend the pipe cleaner in half. Bend the ends back on themselves to make a loop. Bend each end again to make a second loop. Glue the middle of the legs to the back of the oval at the bottom.

4 Fold the triangle of paper in half. Open it out.

5 Fold back a small flap on each side.

6 Snip off the corners that stick out

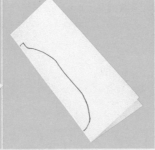

7 Glue the small flaps on the beak on to the middle of the head so that the beak sticks out. Glue on two googly eyes.

8 Fold a piece of A5 coloured paper in half.

9 Draw the shape of half a feather and cut it out.

10 Make cuts along the unfolded edges of the feather, stopping 1cm from the fold.

11 Make two more feathers. Glue them to the back of the parrot behind the feet to make a tail. Glue the craft feathers on to either side of the parrot to make wings. Glue a feather to the top of the head to make plumage. Glue feathers on to the body of the parrot.

12 Attach a loop of string to the back of the head of the parrot with sticky tape. Hang up your colourful parrot.

"Pieces of eight!"

Long John Silver is the one-legged pirate in the book **Treasure Island**. He had a parrot that he named Captain Flint. The parrot sat on Long John Silver's shoulder and was often heard to shriek "Pieces of eight! Pieces of eight!" In fact, pieces of eight were silver coins.

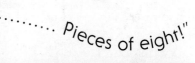

"Pieces of eight!.......... Pieces of eight!"

Into the Deep

Davy Jones' locker is where dead pirates end up – at the bottom of the sea. It is a place full of strange plants and sea creatures. Make this magical underwater scene and fill it with imaginary creatures.

For your underwater scene you will need

- paper
- masking tape
- blue and green paints
- brushes
- bubble wrap
- coloured ink
- drinking straw
- silver foil
- scissors
- glue
- coloured paper
- foam
- wool or ribbon
- googly eyes
- glitter glue

1 Tape a sheet of paper on to a work surface with masking tape. Add water to a blob of blue paint until it is very runny. Paint a watery background on the paper. Let it dry.

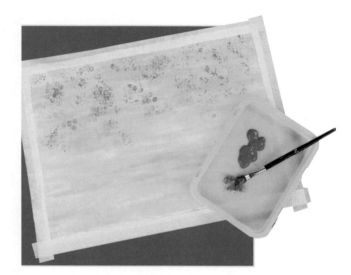

2 Cut some pieces of bubble wrap. Paint the bumpy side of the bubbles. Use the painted side to print bubbles on the paper.

3 Drip blobs of ink on to the paper. Blow through the straw to make weird and wonderful underwater plants.

4 Cut sparkly fish from silver kitchen foil. Glue them on to the picture.

5 Cut out some fish shapes from coloured paper and glue them on to the picture.

6 Cut the top of a jellyfish out of the foam. Cut lengths of wool or ribbon and stick below the jellyfish body. Add googly eyes and decorate with glitter glue.

7 Cut out a star fish from coloured paper. Glue it on to the picture. Decorate with glitter glue.

No one knows all the creatures at the bottom of the sea. You can make up some new creatures of your own.

Meet some sparkly sea creatures in this watery deep-sea scene!

Shipwreck in the Ocean

When pirates were not busy plundering ships they could spend their time making ships inside bottles. You can go one better – impress your crew with this shipwreck scene under rolling ocean waves.

1 Wash the bottle and remove the label. Using the funnel, pour the gravel or sand into the bottle.

To make this ocean shipwreck you will need

- empty clear plastic bottle with tight-fitting lid and a wide neck
- funnel
- handful of colourful gravel (used in fish tanks) or coarse sand
- a few shells
- small plastic toy ship
- jug of water
- cooking oil or baby oil
- blue food colouring

2 Drop the shells and the plastic ship into the bottle.

3 Using the funnel, fill the bottle a quarter of the way up with tap water.

4 Using the funnel, top up the bottle to half full with oil.

5 Add a few drops of blue food colouring. Ask an adult to put the lid on the bottle very tightly.

6 Turn the bottle on its side and rock it gently to see the waves break over the shipwreck. You could rest your bottle on top of a small pile of gravel to stop it rolling away.

Pirate Shipwreck

In April 1717, the **Whydah Gally**, ship of the famous pirate 'Black Sam' Bellamy, sank in a huge storm off Cape Cod, on the coast of North America. The wreck was rediscovered by divers in 1984. Although the ship was thought to be loaded with gold, silver and jewellery when it sank, none was found and divers are still searching for the loot.

To make sure that no water or oil escape from the bottle you could ask an adult to seal the cap with strong glue or a hot glue gun.

Best batten down the hatches – there be a mighty storm brewing!

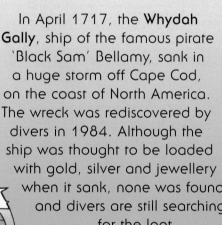

A Pirate Compass

Pirates need a good compass to navigate in the right direction. This handy compass will always tell you which way is north.

For a perfect pirate compass you will need

- needle
- magnet
- pin
- paper
- felt-tip pen
- craft foam
- scissors
- tape or glue
- coloured card
- shallow cereal bowl
- small bowl
- gold and red paper
- glue
- paint
- sticky tape
- jug of water

1 Holding the needle between your thumb and finger, stroke the magnet from the needle tip to the eye about 50 times.

2 Touch the pin with the needle. If the needle has become magnetised, the needle will pick the pin up. If it doesn't, repeat step 1.

3 Using the template on page 31 draw an arrow on to paper. Cut it out. Trace round this paper template on to the foam.

4 Cut out the shape. Attach the needle to the foam with a small piece of tape or a blob of glue.

5 Draw around the shallow cereal bowl on to the card. Cut out 1cm outside the ring you have drawn. Put the small bowl in the middle of the circle. Draw round it. Cut out the inner circle to make a ring.

6 To decorate the ring, cut shapes from gold paper. Cut four diamond shapes from red paper.

7 Glue the shapes on to decorate the ring. Paint spots as shown. Leave to dry. Glue diamonds equally spaced around the ring.

8 Write N, S, E and W on the diamonds (see picture below for the correct order). Put the ring face down and place the cereal bowl on top. Tape the ring to the bowl.

9 Turn the bowl over. Carefully pour some water into the bowl, taking care not to spill any on the ring.

10 Gently place the foam arrow on to the water with the needle on top. When the needle comes to rest, its pointed end will indicate north. Move the dish so that the arrow points to the 'N'.

Weigh anchor, hoist the mizzen and set a new course me hearties!

The First Compass

The earliest compasses were made out of lodestone, a type of magnetic rock. Pirates used compasses to help them navigate dangerous seas and to find hidden treasure.

Templates

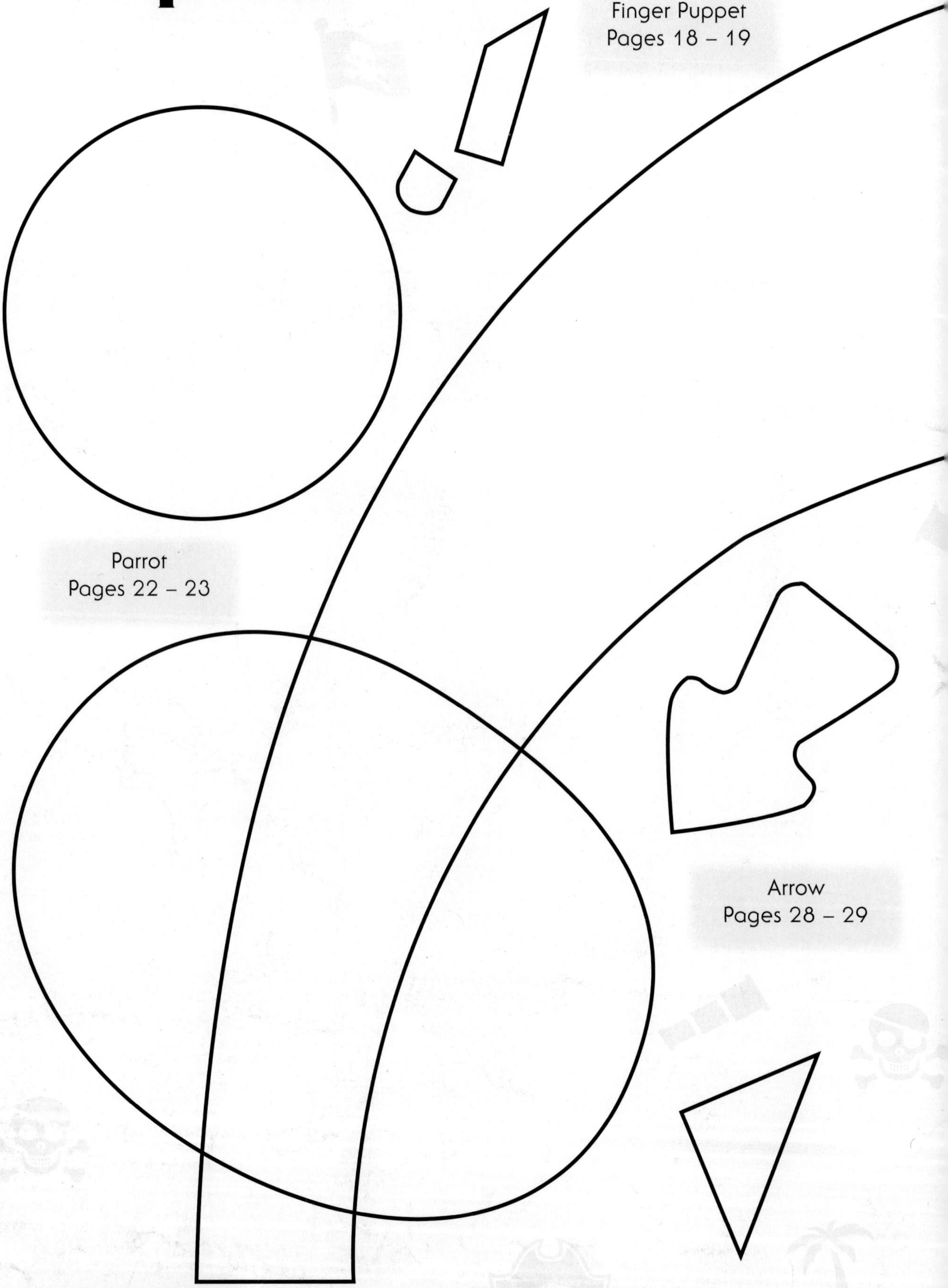

Finger Puppet
Pages 18 – 19

Parrot
Pages 22 – 23

Arrow
Pages 28 – 29

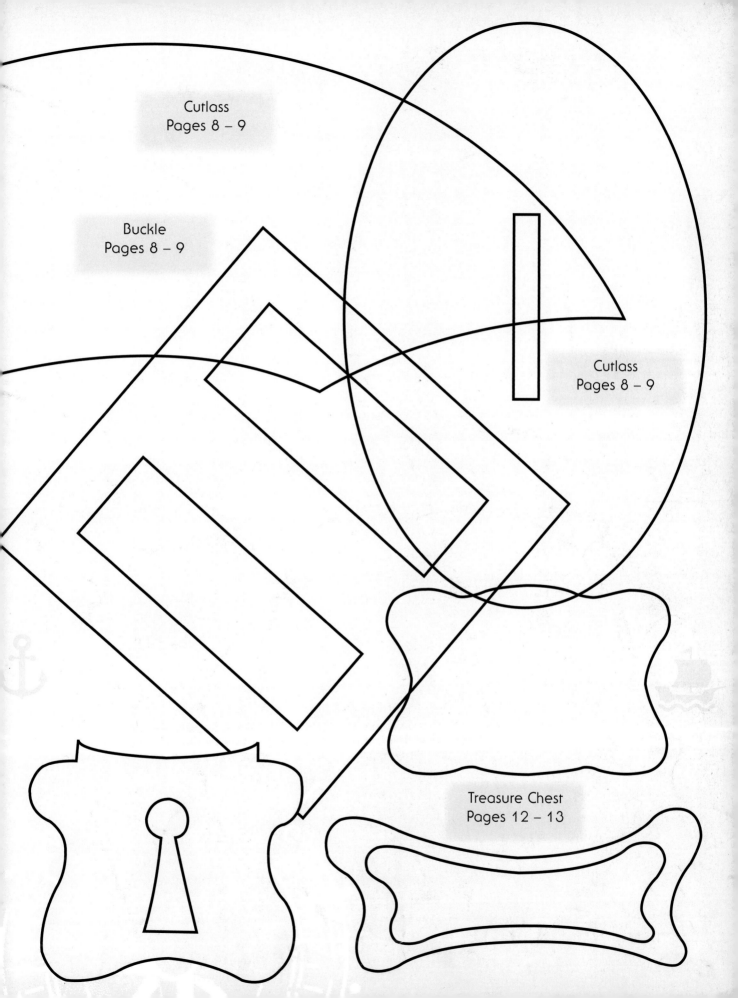

Cutlass
Pages 8 – 9

Buckle
Pages 8 – 9

Cutlass
Pages 8 – 9

Treasure Chest
Pages 12 – 13

Back stitch

Running stitch

  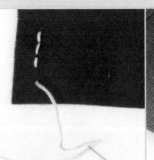 

1 Tie a knot in the end of the thread. Push the needle up from the back of the fabric. Pull the thread through to the knot.

2 Push the needle down through the fabric just behind where it came up. Push the needle up from the back to just in front of the first stitch and pull it through.

3 Push the needle back down to join up with the last stitch. A row of backstitches will all join up together.

1 Follow stage 1 of back stitch. Push the needle back down through the fabric in front of where it came up. Push the point of the needle up through the fabric just in front of where it went down. Pull the thread through. A row of running stitches will have gaps between the stitches.

Further Information

Books

Dressing Up As A: Pirate by Rebekah Shirley (Franklin Watts, 2011)

Up Close: Pirates by Annabelle Lynch (Franklin Watts, 2010)

Websites

www.nationalgeographic.com/pirates

Index

'Black Sam' Bellamy 27
compass 28, 29
cutlass 8, 9, 19
Davy Jones' locker 24
eyepatch 8, 9, 11, 19
finger puppets 18, 19
hardtack 10

Long John Silver 23
octopus 16, 17
parrot 18, 19, 22, 23
pictures 20, 21, 24, 25
pirate clothes 8, 9
Pirates of the Caribbean 4, 21
ship's biscuits 10, 11
shipwreck in a bottle 26, 27

spyglass 6, 7
The Flying Dutchman 21
treasure 12, 13, 29
treasure chest 12, 13, 14, 15
Treasure Island 23
treasure map game 14, 15
tricorne (hat) 4, 5, 9
Whydah Gally 29